I0437368

PLAYING
PEEK A BOO
WITH GOD

PLAYING PEEK A BOO WITH GOD

BASED ON A TRUE STORY

Suzanne Cayce

Outskirts Press, Inc.
Denver, Colorado

The opinions expressed in this manuscript are solely the opinions of the author and do not represent the opinions or thoughts of the publisher. The author has represented and warranted full ownership and/or legal right to publish all the materials in this book.

Playing Peek A Boo With God
Based on a True Story
All Rights Reserved.
Copyright © 2010 Suzanne Cayce
v2.0

This book may not be reproduced, transmitted, or stored in whole or in part by any means, including graphic, electronic, or mechanical without the express written consent of the publisher except in the case of brief quotations embodied in critical articles and reviews.

Outskirts Press, Inc.
http://www.outskirtspress.com

ISBN: 978-1-4327-5169-2

Outskirts Press and the "OP" logo are trademarks belonging to Outskirts Press, Inc.

PRINTED IN THE UNITED STATES OF AMERICA

It is my honor to dedicate this book in loving memory of my husband, Sylvan, who filled 14 wonderful years of my life with more unconditional love, humor, grace, patience, kindness, inspiration, and support than I ever knew was possible. He will forever be my love, my hero, and the wind beneath my wings.

꩜ ꩜ ꩜

Special thanks to Emery Bear for sharing his gift to see beyond this physical reality and translating his visions into beautiful works of art. The image Emery created for the cover of my book is only one example of his extraordinary ability to give us a glimpse into the light of Love. He is widely known for his ability to see and work with angels and has brought those angels to us with the inspired strokes of his paintbrush. You can find more of Emery's enchanting works at www.emerybearart.com.

Contents

CHAPTER ONE

Suzanne stood there, naked, with her troubled gaze fixated on the muddy waters of the pond in front of her. Long, light brown hair hung in tangled disarray around her pale, tear-streaked face. The blue jean shorts, pink tank top, and flimsy under things she had been wearing earlier were lying in a crumpled heap at her feet along with an empty prescription bottle. She had taken the last of her antidepressants. Why? She didn't really know. Perhaps she was trying to find the strength to live or, maybe, the courage to die. She didn't seem to have the answer anymore. However, she was pondering just how far she would have to walk out into those murky waters before they would swallow her up and free her from the nightmare of her life.

The past nine years had been a blur of abuse at the hands of her husband, Wade. His latest tirade had left Suzanne battered, bruised, and unable to convince herself to return home, so she had walked the rough and winding path down to the sprawling pond on their 45-acre Florida homestead.

There was no telling how long Suzanne stood there entrenched in the memories of those horrible years, wondering why, no matter how badly he beat her or how many times he put that gun to her head and threatened her miserable life, she could never seem to find the strength within herself to just leave. Oh, she had tried a couple of times, but the guilt over taking her two children away from their daddy or the fear of trying to raise them on her own always seemed to bring her back.

It wasn't until recently that Suzanne discovered she had not been doing her children any favors by staying in the dysfunctional marriage. She could still remember the moment she realized her little son, Tyler, had come to accept the daily verbal and physical abuse as "normal." In fact, he had become so desensitized to the horror of it all that it was entirely possible that her son would also one day mirror that abuse on someone he loved.

Suzanne's five year old, Tyler, was nothing like he had been at three years of age when, after seeing his Daddy throw her to the ground in a heated rage, he had stared defiantly up at his father and, with tiny fists on his hips, declared, "You hurt my mommy and you hurt my heart."

It seemed Tyler's heart had hardened over the next couple of years and eventually his impudence was aimed at her.

Suzanne remembered him staring without emotion into her worried face as she pleaded with him to help her get his little sister, Nicole, out of the window so that they could escape from his angry father, who was on the other side of the locked bathroom door. Completely unaffected by the tears that mingled with the blood pouring down her face, Tyler had stood like a tiny barrier between her and the window as he stated in a matter of fact voice, "There ain't nothing wrong with you and you ain't leaving my daddy!"

Damn the church for expecting her to continue to honor her marriage vows! To hell with a society that frowns on divorce and makes it difficult for a single parent to survive! Curse the woman stereotype that demanded she suffer in silence and mend whatever was broken! While Suzanne continued to endure in this abusive and dysfunctional relationship, her children were learning how to be, and the odds that they would become the next generation of abusers or the abused were becoming greater with every moment she continued to stay.

Suzanne would never remember what force pulled her away from the pond that day, but there was a sudden and very marked shift that overtook her. With a flip of her hair, a strong, confident woman turned and walked away. She was still naked as she made her way up the narrow path that wound its way along the cornfield and toward the house. Walking cautiously around the back of the old, weather worn barn she quickly surveyed the driveway looking for any sign of a vehicle or if someone was home. Feeling that the coast was clear, she ran swiftly toward the back door of the ranch style, brick home and let herself in. Making a beeline for the master bedroom, she quickly rummaged through the dresser drawers as she mumbled to herself. "Ew, who picked this stuff out? The woman has absolutely no taste."

Finally, she settled on a pair of cut off shorts and a red cotton top that was loosely laced together down the front to reveal her ample cleavage and navel. As she slipped into tennis shoes and grabbed a handful of change and small bills that were scattered on top of the dresser, she barely glanced at the photos of the little boy and girl displayed there. In fact, there was no indication that she recognized who the children were. Without even a backward glance, she walked out of the door and then kept on walking, right out of their lives.

It was days later and thousands of miles away from anything remotely familiar when Suzanne started to come back into focus. She felt herself being shaken awake and a male voice that she didn't recognize was saying, "Lisa, Lisa! You need to wake up now. We're in Vegas. This is where you wanted to go and I have to keep on moving if I'm going to get this load delivered on time."

Rousing from a deep sleep, Suzanne tried to regain her bearings. A quick survey of her surroundings made it clear that she was in the sleeper of a semi truck, but Suzanne had no idea how she had gotten there or who the short, sandy haired man standing in front of her was or why he was calling her Lisa. Even more disturbing was the fact that apparently she was in Las Vegas and she had absolutely no recollection of how she had gotten there.

Trying to remain calm, Suzanne smiled at the strange man in front of her and apologized for holding him up. "Let me just get my stuff together and I'll be out of your way."

"You didn't bring anything with you," he said impatiently.

"Oh yeah, that's right. I like to travel light." Suzanne was surprisingly quick with her response as she tried desperately to hide the fear and confusion gathering in her mind like a summer storm from out of nowhere.

In an attempt to gain some composure, she smoothed her hair with one hand while the other hand went absentmindedly to the pocket of her blue jean shorts. To her surprise, it was empty except for a couple of loose coins. Panicked, she quickly searched her other pockets only to find the same bareness. "My God," she screamed silently. "How did I get here? What am I going to do?"

Somehow, despite her extreme anxiety in the moment, Suzanne found the courage to turn to the man, who probably already felt like he had gone out of his way to help her out, and asked him if he wouldn't mind spotting her a twenty. "I must have lost the little bit of money I did have," she said apologetically, "but, if you'll write your address down, I'll be sure to send it back to you." Her voice had become pleading at this point.

Almost reluctantly, he reached into his back pocket and handed her a twenty from his wallet. It was obvious he wanted to be moving on and the only thing standing between him and the open road was her outstretched hand.

Suzanne's gratitude showed in her smile and she reached across to this stranger and gave him a quick hug. "You have no idea how much this means to me," she gushed.

As she turned away and walked slowly across the huge parking lot of the Flying K, Suzanne weighed her almost nonexistent options. She decided that her best course of action at the moment would probably be to take advantage of the facilities in the truck stop and try to regain her bearings while she figured out what to do next. She stopped by the front counter to spend a precious $1.19 on a comb and then headed for the only sanctuary available to her in that moment, the ladies room.

The mirror that covered an entire wall above the sinks brought Suzanne to a sudden halt. "Oh my God! Oh my God!" Her shock, disbelief, horror, and total confusion found no expression other then another "Oh my God!" Suzanne's formerly brown hair was now a brilliant strawberry blonde. The extremely revealing top and Daisy Duke blue jean shorts she was wearing had been buried at the bottom of her dresser drawer for over a year. Suzanne had not worn that outfit since the horrific night when she had tried, unconvincingly, to keep one of the patrons at the bar she moonlighted at from having any more to drink. He had persuaded her to give him "just one more," after which he had left and apparently gone home where he fell asleep with a lit cigarette and burned to death. Feeling as if she had contributed to his demise in some way, Suzanne had immediately quit that job. Over the next year, the flimsy cotton top, cut off shorts, and the devastating memory had worked their way out of sight, but now there they were, reflecting back at her, taunting her. What horrible thing had she done this time? Was she responsible for contributing to yet another death? That question released a tirade of other questions. Her children, were they okay? If she was in Vegas, how many miles was she away from her home in Florida? How could she have gotten there without any memory of the journey? The time? The date? How could she call home? Did she want to call home? Why couldn't she remember?

Suzanne took one more look at the image staring back at her from the mirror. "Okay girl, you have got to get your shit together," she told herself firmly.

First things first, she had to get her hair combed and wash her face so she didn't look like the bedraggled homeless person she apparently was at the moment. The next thing, Suzanne decided, was that she would go by the newspaper rack and check the date. She would not call home since her children were too young to answer the phone and, if things were the way she had left them, she could only expect to be greeted by rage from her husband. She didn't have the courage for that or, for all she knew, possibly something even worse.

On her way out of the bathroom, Suzanne noticed a bulletin board covered with flyers of missing women and children. She paused for a moment to look for her own picture. She still didn't know how long she had been gone.

She was thankful to find a daily paper that someone had left behind on the counter of the bar in the truck stop restaurant, but when she glanced at the date on the top of the page, her devastation returned. June 3, 1995? Three days? How could so much time just disappear like a dreamless night of sleep? What had happened in the last 72 hours? "God, please, I need to remember," she begged.

Even though she was completely overwhelmed almost to the point of panic by her reality, somehow she managed to maintain enough composure to order a cup of coffee. She turned to the classified section of the newspaper. It was unlikely that she would find the answers to her problems there amongst all those ads, but perhaps the brief distraction would help her creative mind come up with some unexpected solutions. The only sign of her inner turmoil was a solitary tear that rolled out of the corner of her eye and meandered down her cheek. Little did she know, that precious tear would be her salvation.

"What's a pretty thing like you doing with tears on your face?"

Suzanne turned and smiled weakly up at the handsome stranger as he sat down beside her and motioned to the waitress for a cup of java. He was at least six feet tall with tousled blond hair and a big, bright smile. "It's a long story," Suzanne said with a sigh.

"Well, I hate to see anyone crying. Is there something I can do to make you smile?"

Normally, Suzanne was not one to share her troubles with a perfect stranger, but these circumstances called for exceptions. "Well, if you could give me a job that includes room and board so I can make enough money to get back to my home in Florida, that would really make me happy." Suzanne ended with a wry smile. She knew that even though a job like the one she had just stated was exactly what she needed, it would take an incredible miracle for her to find it.

She watched as the friendly stranger beside her stared thoughtfully into his coffee for a few moments and then turned to her and began to speak. "You know, I'm a truck driver and I don't live here. I actually live in Fallbrook, California. That is even further away from Florida than Las Vegas, so I don't know if you would even be interested in what I can offer you. My wife just went through surgery and, with me being gone so much, I'm sure she could use some help around the house until she gets back on her feet. We wouldn't be able to offer you any pay, just a room and your meals. With her being sick lately, money has been a little tight. You wouldn't have to do much, just the basic housekeeping, feed the cats, and cook some meals. You should have plenty of free time to go out and find another job where you can earn the money you need to get back to Florida. In the meantime, you would have a roof over your head and you won't be hungry. I know it's not much…" his voice trailed off.

Suzanne could hardly believe what she was hearing. Yes, it was further away from Florida, but she had no other options at that point and the sun was starting to sink lower toward the western horizon. A hot meal and a bed in a home in California sounded a whole lot better than the many unknowns she was facing on the streets in Las Vegas. "If you're serious about your offer, I'd love to take you up on it!"

"You understand this is just temporary, right? It will just be until my wife recovers from surgery."

"Yes, yes! I understand and I promise to do my very best to help your wife and take care of your home. This really means a lot to me. I can't thank you enough! Oh, by the way, my name is Suzanne." She stuck her hand out and gave his a firm, friendly shake.

"I'm Doug." He paused for a moment and then continued, "Well, if you're certain this is what you want, we're going to have to head out if we're going to get home tonight. Where are your bags?"

"Um," Suzanne hesitated, "no bags, just me. Is that okay?"

Doug raised his right eyebrow. "I probably don't want to know," he commented. "Well, I'm sure my wife can direct you to a secondhand store. You're going to need some different clothes."

"That would be great," Suzanne said quietly, grateful that he didn't question her any further on her absence of luggage.

Her arrival in Fallbrook, CA was a little tense. Doug's wife, Karen, didn't seem to know how to react to her new scantily clad housekeeper. While it was apparent that she was grateful for the extra help around the house, it also appeared that she was very suspicious of Suzanne and her husband's motivation for picking up a beautiful stranger to be her caregiver.

Anxious to please and to erase any doubt, Suzanne spent many hours meticulously cleaning every nook and cranny of the large two story home and taking care of any other household responsibilities. She used only a few hours in the afternoon to attend to her immediate personal needs. The first, of course, was to obtain some clothes from a local secondhand store with some of what remained of the $20.00 she had been given. Thankfully, she was able to get a couple of bags full for just $5.00 each. Afterwards, she put in applications at all the stores and businesses within walking distance of her new home. But most of the managers or owners just shook their heads and said they had no positions available at the time.

On the verge of despair but refusing to give up, Suzanne walked through the door of a local cocktail lounge. She had sworn she would never put herself in the position of serving alcohol again, yet, for some reason, there she was, smiling and assuring the owner she would do an awesome job for him if he would just give her the opportunity.

"I'm shorthanded for the next three nights if you are willing work them. It will give me an opportunity to evaluate your performance and determine if you are someone I could use on a more permanent basis. For now, all I can offer you is the next three nights. Take it or leave it." Ron was a little gruff, but Suzanne was so ecstatic to have any job, even if it was just for a few nights, so she barely noticed.

Karen was fine with Suzanne being gone in the evenings. She usually took her pain meds and went to bed early, and she didn't require any assistance during the night. So, although she would have preferred another job, it seemed that her new cocktail waitress position would provide the income she so desperately needed to get back to her children and her home.

Suzanne spent her first ten dollars of tip money on a calling card and then made a phone call to the church she had attended in Florida, hoping for some help and words of advice and encouragement. However, because of her huge memory gap, her story was met with skepticism, and the most that was promised was that her case would be presented at the next church meeting. Then they would determine what, if anything, they could do to help her. She was told that her children were in the care of one of the church elders and his family because Wade was unable to care for them and work too. She also learned that Wade had been under suspicion for murder since her disappearance. In their attempt to find out what had happened to Suzanne, the police had pulled up several restraining orders that she had placed against her husband in the past, and they were suspecting domestic violence. So, of course, the pastor was happy and relieved to know where Suzanne was and that she was okay. He also promised to pass this news on to those who needed to know or were concerned. After Suzanne obtained the phone number for the residence where her children were staying, she thanked the pastor and hung up.

The sweet voices of her two children, Tyler and Nicole, brought a flood of tears to Suzanne's eyes. There was no way to explain to her babies how she had gotten so far away from them or why she didn't know when she would be able to see them again. She did her best to assure them she would have them back in her arms very soon and she couldn't wait to hold them and smother them with kisses and hugs. She reminded them repeatedly that she loved them and hoped somehow, someway, that love would span the time and distance between them and bring them comfort. But, for her, there was only an empty, desperate yearning for a reunion that couldn't happen soon enough. With renewed determination to make it happen quickly, she prepared for work.

Her shift that evening seemed uneventful except for one very memorable incident. Looking back later, Suzanne would state that she was certain some divine plan had been set in motion days, weeks, years, or possibly even a lifetime before bringing her to that one pivotal moment; the moment a certain male customer raised the drink she had just given him to his lips.

"I ordered Diet Coke and I believe this is regular Coke." The handsome, middle-aged man handed his drink back to her.

"I am so sorry!" Suzanne apologized with an embarrassed smile. "What is your name?"

"It's Kent."

"Kent, I'll take care of this right away."

As quickly as possible, Suzanne returned with the correct drink and apologized once again.

"It's fine." His smile was gracious and he had a mischievous twinkle in his eyes as he continued, "In fact, just to show that I completely forgive you, let me take you out to eat when you get off."

"The smartest thing you could ever do is just walk out of here and forget you ever saw me, because I'm nothing but trouble," Suzanne retorted with a smile.

"Why don't you give me the opportunity to make that judgment for myself once I get to know you a little better?" Again, Suzanne resisted, but once more Kent insisted. Finally, won over by his charm and still feeling like she needed to make amends for messing up his drink order, she gave in. "Alright, just a cup of coffee," she conceded.

"Coffee it is." He grinned.

Their conversation over that cup of coffee during the wee hours of the morning continued until dawn. Never before had she felt such grace and acceptance from another man. Dark, long, wavy locks framed his face, which had warmth and sincerity etched in every handsome line. Suzanne was mesmerized by the smile that seemed to hover constantly within the depths of his eyes and frequently found its way beneath his thick mustache. As vulnerable as she was, Suzanne felt safe with Kent. There was also this strange familiarity between them, almost as if they had known each other before.

They continued to connect as Kent drove her up winding mountain roads to an overlook. Together they watched the sun peek out at the edge of the expansive valley below and then boldly splash the skies around it in vivid hues of pink and orange as it rose to greet a new day. Kent and Suzanne breathed deeply, inhaling the fresh mountain air and the fragrant perfume of the wildflowers that surrounded them and, for the first time in years, Suzanne found herself laughing. Kent's sense of humor was never-ending, and dormant joy seemed to awaken and bubble up inside of her, spilling out in uncontrollable giggles of pleasure. The entire experience was one of rebirth for her. She knew in those moments that she could never go back to the unhappiness of her marriage.

After returning to check in with Karen and ensuring that her needs were addressed, Kent and Suzanne decided to put together a picnic and escape to the local park. Under the shade of large live oak trees they continued to discover each other and be amazed at how much they had in common, even though Kent was almost 16 years her senior. Both were delighted to have found this new, quickly developing friendship.

A phone call that Suzanne received later that evening would bring her time with Kent to a rapid end. The church she had contacted earlier had agreed to pay for her flight home. Although Suzanne had been thrilled by their immediate solution, she also knew there would be a conference with the church elders when she returned, and that was something she dreaded. But, in that moment, the only thing that mattered was that she would soon have her children back in her arms.

After sharing her news with Kent, she asked this wonderful man whom she had just met to take her on the necessary two-hour drive to the regional airport the next day. His response had taken her completely by surprise. The look on his face was one of utter disappointment and sadness. In fact, Suzanne swore she could even see tears welling up in his eyes as he told her that he knew he was going to have to let her go, but he just didn't realize it was going to be so soon. She couldn't ever remember someone actually caring whether she stayed or went, except for her babies, so this was new to her.

Suzanne spent the rest of the evening wrapping up her other commitments. Karen had gotten used to having Suzanne around and was sorry to see her go; however, she assured Suzanne, she was doing much better and she would be able to manage. Ron told Suzanne he was thankful she was able to help him out in a jam and if she was ever in the area again and needed a job, he would love to have her back.

The next day, the drive to the airport was punctuated with silence as both Suzanne and Kent tried to make sense of how something so wonderful seemed to be coming to an end as quickly as it had begun. As they said their goodbyes, both cursed the thousands of miles that would soon separate them, but they promised to stay in touch. Kent insured this by handing Suzanne a calling card with an insane amount of minutes on it and made her swear she would call him as soon as her plane touched down in Florida.

On the flight home, Suzanne relived each precious moment she had shared with Kent. She began to realize that the happiness and peace she experienced with him had made the horrors of her marriage even more apparent. How could she continue to expose her children to such a hostile environment? It had to stop! She needed to end her marriage and remove her children from all the chaos and turmoil. Suzanne only wished she had found the courage to do it sooner because she was beginning to understand clearly what was meant by the sins of the father being passed on for generations. Children only know what they live, and they either go on to imitate some exaggerated form of what they experienced, or they choose to reject it completely, usually going to an opposite extreme. Why hadn't she acknowledged this earlier and saved her son and daughter? Why? Perhaps it was because she too was a product of dysfunction.

The sins of her father had been imbedded deep within her. She had seen this truth at a very early age when, after her dad had brutally beaten her again for some unknown reason, she had taken her hurt and anger out on a cow that had dared to switch her with its tail when she stooped down to milk it. As Suzanne pummeled the cow with her fists, there was a moment of recognition; she had the monster inside of her too! She had sworn to never have children in that moment because she feared she would be just like her father, unable to control that raging beast. She had been somewhat relieved by the three miscarriages she had suffered before her children were born. Suzanne figured that God must have been saving the babies from her. When Tyler and Nicole finally arrived in her life, she lived in fear of that monster. What if she couldn't control it? What if she hurt her children the way her father had hurt her? There were many times when she could feel it seething inside of her. Suzanne was always aware it was there, so she always kept a tight rein on the beast, rarely disciplining her children at all. Despite her best efforts, once or twice, it found its way out and reminded her that it was still alive by an angry hand mark or welt on her child's tender skin. Sadly, she had been so intent on saving her children from the beast within her that, somehow, she managed to overlook the one that ran rampant through their lives on a daily basis and told them twisted tales of how it was okay for daddies to hurt mommies with angry words and fists.

When Suzanne got back to Florida, her resolve to maintain a safe distance from her husband was made possible by one of her dearest friends, Bea, who immediately opened her home to Suzanne and her children and protected them like a lioness shelters her cubs.

Later, she found the courage necessary to tell the elders of the church that even though she realized they would probably excommunicate her and pray for her damned soul, she could not find it within herself to ever return to her home or her marriage. She honestly felt like she had already lived in hell for the past nine years, and frankly she needed a small reprieve before her final doom.

Kent's friendship became a stabilizing force for Suzanne. His daily phone calls and the cards he sent on a regular basis seemed to give her strength. She could feel her soul begin to breathe again under his nurturing care, and her spirit blossomed with renewed confidence as she began the process of filing for divorce.

The paperwork was not pretty, just a fill in the blank form provided by the court, but it was inexpensive and very quick. To insure her husband, Wade, did not contest the divorce, Suzanne gave up all three homes that they owned as well as all other assets except a car and few small personal items. Her only hard stance, which ultimately met with no resistance at all from Wade, was that she would be the custodial parent of Tyler and Nicole. Those days found her treasuring her sanity and a peaceful and safe environment for her children to thrive in above any material possessions. Less than two months later, her divorce was finalized.

Feeling that the greatest obstacle that kept him from being with Suzanne had been removed; Kent immediately boarded a flight on the silver-winged bird that would bring them back together again. Undaunted by the things that would have caused most men who had only met a woman a couple months prior to pause, Kent asked Suzanne to marry him as soon as he got off the plane. Even more surprising, this woman, whose experience of marriage had been less than wonderful, agreed to be his wife without even the slightest hesitation.

On August 1, 1995, wearing jeans and tee shirts, in a simple, quiet ceremony in front of the local justice of the peace, Suzanne and Kent pledged their lives to each other.

There was no bouquet to toss, no bridesmaid to catch it, no cake to cut, and no gifts to open other than a promotional package of laundry detergent and dryer sheet samples the clerk of the court handed them. None of those things mattered to Kent and Suzanne. Their joy in that moment did not have its roots in anything material; they only felt the bliss of two souls that had found each other and promised to never lose each other again.

A year before the wheels of fate had brought Kent and Suzanne together, someone had asked little Tyler where he went to school. "You go to California and then you take a left," was his innocently prophetic reply.

California was a beautiful place for their new beginning. However, a year later, the declining health of Suzanne's parents brought her and her family back to the South, this time to Mississippi where her parents had retired. They had wanted to escape the harsh winters of Wisconsin, and a place where it was possible to grow a garden year-round had intrigued them.

While Suzanne's relationship with her parents was tense, at

best, she remained optimistic and always hoped for something better. Being near them and able to help them out made her feel that she was at least making an effort and, hopefully, she wouldn't have any regrets later in her life.

If you happened to peek in on Suzanne, Kent, Tyler, and Nicole over the next couple of years, you would find quiet contentment. Kent had settled into a job as a foreman at a local factory and, while it may not have been his perfect choice for a career, the benefits were great for his newly expanded family. The added income combined with his naval retirement made for a comfortable living. Suzanne kept herself busy running her ever-expanding housekeeping business and caring for the children.

It would have been easy to end their story with "and they lived happily ever after," except for one ripple in Suzanne's otherwise tranquil existence--an increasing, constant, nagging physical pain that interrupted her days and nights and interfered with her ability to work. In time, the torture spread to her mind.

CHAPTER TWO

There was no one home on that rainy, dismal day in October, just a vacant shell of a woman. The welcoming light in Suzanne's eyes that once sent out a playful invitation had long since been shuttered over by murky layers of pain. Embers of joy, that had once danced brightly in a spirit filled with enthusiasm for life, now lay cold and dormant, a miserable reminder of better days. Worst of all, Suzanne's mind, once clear and dazzling with brilliance, had become a jumbled and twisted mass of confusion. The evil terror of despair had reached within the very bowels of her soul and seemed to hover there, taunting her with an endless array of unanswered questions.

Suzanne looked around the stark, clinical room where she was confined as if by some miracle she would be able to find some answers written there on the bare, impersonal, gray walls. Nothing. There wasn't anything there except silence and perfect order. Everything was in its designated place. There was a single hospital bed clothed with crisp white sheets neatly and tightly tucked by some disciplined orderly. A simple nightstand with two functional drawers stood next to the bed. A small, metal desk stood in the corner, and the only other furniture was the hard, unforgiving chair upon which she sat. But the simplicity surrounding

Suzanne only served to emphasize the chaos within her.

Her mind was like a field filled with treacherous land mines, exploding at random with brutal questions that bombarded her incessantly. "Why, God, why?" she screamed in silent agony. "Where did it all go wrong? How can I find peace amongst all this insanity? Why am I here in this place, this horrendous nightmare of a place, where nothing makes sense anymore? Why are all my dreams being snatched away one by one and shattered like useless fragments of glass along the byways of my life? Why? Why? Why! Where are you, God?" Her cries had almost become defiant.

She had never doubted that there was a God, something or someone much greater than herself; she only questioned where this being was. She was always sure that this higher power had created her, but she wondered why. She had never disputed that there was some divine plan for her existence; she just didn't know what it was. She had never doubted God, or had she?

Gnawing pain that coursed incessantly throughout her entire body forced Suzanne to struggle out of her chair. She stood for a moment, looked despondently around her cramped quarters, and then walked stiffly into the adjoining bathroom. The image in the mirror over the cold white porcelain sink seemed to lure her. Staring at the sad woman in the reflection, she felt as though she was observing a stranger. Haunting blue eyes highlighted her beautiful pale face. Her soft, full mouth was fixed in a sullen frown, something she didn't have to strength to change at that moment. It was hard to believe that she was only thirty-two. Staring deep into her own vacant eyes, she screamed, "Where have you gone?" She could have been asking the question of herself or of God; she wasn't sure. The only thing abundantly clear was that neither one of them appeared to be visible in that mirror.

Suzanne turned away and felt an overwhelming sadness for the woman she had known herself to be. She wondered what had become of her. Tears began to spill unchecked down her ashen cheeks as she returned to her room and fell across the hard, uncomfortable bed she had been forced to sleep upon for the past few nights. Mercifully, memories of the previous days and nights were foggy at best. She was only beginning to become aware of why she was confined to the place, a hospital for the insane. To her, it was just a fancy prison. They had taken away all of her personal belongings along with the freedoms and privileges she had come to take for granted. Cameras in the corners of her room made no secret of the fact that her every move was observed. The white coats came and went quietly, prodding, poking, taking blood, and dispensing little paper cups filled with multicolored pills. For the most part, it had all been a blur, especially since each dose of medicine was followed by hours of dreamless sleep. Oh, how sleep had been welcomed! It had evaded her for longer than she could recall, and if there was some serenity to be found amongst all the uncertainty in her life, it came only during those quiet hours of nothingness.

Fibromyalgia was her fateful diagnosis. Her doctor had told her that this word explained the crippling, blinding pain that had invaded her life, making sleep illusive and suicide an appealing option. So, it had a name, this destructive force that had taken the very best of her. Her brilliant smile and quick wit and her love for poetry, laughter, and life were all buried deep within the pain of this monster. It was little consolation that she had not given up without a valiant fight. She had battled bravely in the face of the relentless brute for two years before the pain finally conquered her spirit and overcame her will to live. But, any mountain, if chiseled away at long enough, is bound to crumble, so Suzanne lay there wondering if she could find the strength and courage within herself or if perhaps God cared enough to help her pick up the slivered shards of her life and put them back together again. Like a child playing hide-and-seek, she lifted her eyes toward heaven and whispered, "Where are you?"

The answer came softer than a baby's sigh, filling her heart with sweet joy. "I am right here. I will never leave you!"

She didn't stop to question the origin of those comforting words; her heart knew. For the first time in many days, her lips curved upward into a relaxed smile and a quiet peace enveloped her soul. "Thank you," she mumbled sleepily, "Sometimes I just need to be reminded."

The sun peeped shyly through a small crack at the edge of the heavy draperies and signaled the dawn of a new day. As her eyes opened, Suzanne looked around the dismal room that had unfortunately become much too familiar.

It was customary for Suzanne to start her day with a silent prayer of gratitude, but lately she had struggled to find even the simplest things to be thankful for. Remembering the words that had soothed her soul the night before, she thanked God for always being there for her, and she was extremely grateful to have been able to sleep through the previous night. "One more thing, as long as I've got you on the line," she added, "What is with all this now you see me, now you don't? Are we playing peek-a-boo?" That thought delighted Suzanne immensely. As she arose out of bed, a small laugh escaped her lips.

Already, the desolation and desperation that had encompassed her on previous days were beginning to fade away. The genesis of this day brought with it refreshed strength, an abundance of hope, and, if you looked closely, you could see a glimmer of light breaking through the darkness in her eyes. She didn't understand how precious that sparkle in her eyes was to her two children, who were once again out of reach, added to the list of treasures that had been torn away from her. She didn't understand what they meant when they would say, "Mommy, we wish you would come back to us."

"I am right here," she would absentmindedly reply, "I haven't gone anywhere."

A small paper heart on the otherwise empty desk caught her attention. As she must have done a hundred times before, she lovingly picked it up and hugged it to her breast. She didn't know exactly how it had come to be there but she had found comfort in the simple message scrawled across its tattered face in bright red crayon, "We love you, Mommy."

A tear rolled down her cheek and splashed among the other tear stains, which were now only dried reminders of other moments like these when her heart ached to be reunited with her babies, Nicole and Tyler. She was being denied simple pleasures like hugs that only reached her waist and bubble monsters made at bath time all because, somewhere along the way, amidst the sleepless nights filled with excruciating pain, she had lost control.

She could still see their bewildered faces looking up at her and questioning what was wrong with their mommy. Of course, she had assured them that "all is well." How out of character! Suzanne would have never said, "All is well." She didn't know whether she had been trying to fool herself or her children. The only certain thing was that she had been steadily falling apart inside. The voices in her head had become louder and more insistent, and with each agonizing moment that her physical distress robbed her of much needed sleep, she weakened. Finally, too exhausted to fight, she allowed "them" to take control. Caressing the simple paper heart, she knew that all was not well!

Suzanne was brought out of her musings by the sound of the heavy metal door to her room opening. A tall, slender woman entered. The white coat was not necessary; she carried herself with the confident air of a doctor. Her short, dark brown tresses were smoothed to perfection and the small, silver-framed glasses that perched precariously on the end of her long, thin nose added the finishing touch to her flawless appearance. Her smile was narrow and lacked warmth.

"How are you today, Suzanne?" the doctor asked.

"Better, I think."

Suzanne sat down warily on her rumpled bed and tried not to look too uncomfortable, but she must have been unable to hide the questioning look on her face.

"You don't remember me, Suzanne?" quizzed the doctor.

Suzanne's mind went into overdrive. If she was supposed to remember this doctor, it must mean that they had met before. *Think. Think. Think!* She scolded herself silently. *God, come on, I don't need to look like a total nutcase in front of this woman!*

Her quick mental search brought up absolutely nothing. It was still all a complete fog. Perhaps this woman was the one who had sat silently at her bedside. Suzanne remembered waking slightly from a drugged sleep to see someone quietly observing her. In any case, it seemed that except for a few fleeting memories, the past few days were not to be recalled, and this doctor did not seem to be among the scattered remnants. Suzanne smiled apologetically at the doctor. "I'm sorry. I am terrible when it comes to remembering names, perhaps you could tell me yours again."

"I understand," the doctor replied, "My name is Dr. Polland."

"I'll try to remember this time, Dr. Polland." Suzanne smiled warmly and hoped she had somehow managed to cover up the real reason she had no recollection of this woman. "Actually, you do seem to be doing a lot better this morning, Suzanne. I am happy to see you up and about, which alone is a wonderful improvement. Do you feel up to answering some questions?"

Of course she didn't, but somehow Suzanne felt like she really didn't have any choice in the matter. Her only response was a slight shrug.

The questions came in rapid succession, but no matter how probing they became, the doctor remained aloof and impersonal. She didn't seem to understand that with every question yet another horrible memory had to be dragged into the spotlight and relived. What was wrong with this doctor? Didn't she know that when she closed the door behind her, Suzanne would be left there, surrounded by all those foreboding bundles she had once hidden away so carefully in the darkened recesses of her mind? Why must she be faced with the task of tucking them away again? Why was this doctor doing this to her?

"She is just trying to help you, Suzanne." She heard a gentle voice within her mind. "Try to keep calm and answer the questions. I will help you."

"You tried to help me before and look where it got me!" Suzanne screamed silently at the voice.

"If we hadn't helped you, you would be dead! You're an ungrateful bitch," said another voice that only she could hear.

"Shut up! Will you all just shut up?" Suzanne's plea was once again silent. She looked at the doctor with an apologetic smile. "I am so sorry, Doctor. I am having trouble concentrating this morning. What did you say?" This time, Suzanne spoke aloud.

The barrage of questions finally ended. Just as Suzanne had predicted earlier, the doctor exited without even a backward glance. If she had bothered looking back, she would have seen that the smile on Suzanne's face, one placed there expressly for the doctor's benefit, had faded into a look of despair. Silent pleas for help were being issued in a heavenly direction because Suzanne knew that she was not strong enough to complete the chore that lie before her alone. All those hideous memories, exposed to the naked light of day, had to be buried once again! However, she must take care to wrap each one perfectly, so if she happened to stumble across them in the future, perhaps the love and care with which she took to gently pack them away would somehow diminish the effects of what was inside. The most difficult ones must be taken care of first while she still had the fortitude.

Her father had the most packages and they required the greatest of care. She had learned from previous experiences that it was very important to cover each dark memory with one of light and love. So, reluctantly, she began as pictures from days gone by played on and on like a relentless horror flick.

Her father was very angry again. She didn't know why; she rarely did. She had done everything exactly as he had told her, but, as always, she must have somehow failed. His hands felt like cold steel bands as they clenched around her scrawny arms and he threw her onto the dirty cement floor of the barn. She was thankful for the little bit of straw under her head and she prayed that it would cushion the blows. She knew what came next before he even reached to ensnare her golden locks in his large fist, and this time was no exception. Once again, she experienced the agony of her head being slammed repeatedly into the hard, unyielding concrete. The pain was excruciating, but the anguish in her heart was far greater at that moment, for she had dared to look up into his eyes. The fiery anger within their icy blue depths was enough to send a chill throughout her entire being. His perfect teeth were clenched like a rabid dog and, to her horror; he had grabbed a shovel that had been leaning against a wall just within his reach. As he raised the rusted tool above his head, she remembered thinking that it was probably the last time she would ever have to endure her father's wrath. Death would have been a welcome escape from all the abuse, but then he had stopped unexpectedly. His face softened and he stooped to gently pick her up. Suzanne winced as his hand came up from behind him toward her face before she realized he was holding his tattered red handkerchief. He wiped the tears away, and later, with the same worn hankie and some cold water drawn from an outdoor tap, he removed the blood. It was then that he had said, "I love you." She had never heard those words spoken from his lips before, and she hung onto them like a final breath, a sprinkle of sunshine in with the darkness.

Suzanne would have loved to find some fast-forward or erase buttons to help get her past the poignant images that had been released, but instead she found herself face to face with horrors that looped in an endless replay Hell.

Over and over again, she relived the suffocating minutes when her father had forced her face into that foam pillow while his other fist, hard and unrelenting, rained down blow upon stinging blow to her back. Once again, she had felt her life slipping away. She had not been struggling against her father, as she was sure he was convinced. She was just fighting to breathe!

Her mom had saved her life that day. It was the only time she could ever recall her mother, who always seemed to be distant and out of touch, interfering on her behalf. Maybe it was the sight of her daughter's face turning a bluish hue that prompted her. Whatever it was, her mother had taken the next several blows for Suzanne as her father continued to rage. He pushed her mother out of the way and ripped her dress completely down the front. Horrified by it all but thankful to be able to breathe again, Suzanne had broken free and escaped.

The sprinkles of light and love were hard to come by, but she could always throw in some popcorn. That was the only thing that ever seemed to bring her father and her together--their love for popcorn. She had many memories of nights sitting by his side sharing the largest bowl of popcorn ever. They never really talked; they just sat there next to each other dipping silently into the golden kernels that were dripping with butter and dusted lightly with salt. A love for popcorn was their only bond. A weak smile touched her lips as she thought of using popcorn for packing material. How ingenious!

It seemed so ironic to her that a child could be raised in a "Christian home" and yet be starved for any memory of love. The only god she had been taught about seemed to be a very furious god. She pictured him to be an awful lot like her own father. It seemed impossible to ever appease this god. The long lists of "thou shalls" and "thou shall nots" spelled out certain damnation for her because, like her father's many rules, she knew she could never figure them all out or even begin to get them right.

Suzanne raced through the remaining memories, tucking them away one by one. All of those times when Daddy called her a whore even though her virginity was still intact were packed away with vague recollections of him rocking gently in his favorite chair and playing sweet hymns on his shiny harmonica.

The countless times that he told her she could do nothing right and that she was absolutely no good for anything were covered softly with memories of those rare times when he would doodle little pictures for her on a scrap of paper. There was that one cold winter evening when he had allowed her to ride with him down their sloping, snow-packed driveway on a little white sled. That memory served as a perfect cushion for all of the swollen, bruised, and broken lips and black eyes.

Suzanne continued sorting and sifting, struggling to find those moments of love and laughter to place amongst the darkness. Still, there were various times when she had no choice but to fall back on old faithful, that big oversized bowl filled with light, fluffy pieces of popcorn.

The voices in her head were silent now except for the muffled crying of a small child.

CHAPTER THREE

There was a quick rap-tap-tap on the door that announced the young gentleman, but in a moment Suzanne realized that he had gone as quickly as he had come. Judging by the rapid knocks she could hear on adjacent doors, she figured his mission had been simply to let her and everyone else know that is was lunchtime.

Lunch sounded extremely good to her. She couldn't remember eating in days. She did have a vague recollection of someone setting a hot plate of food on the desk in her room one evening. She had been very hungry then too, but just as she had uncovered the plate, she looked back toward her bed and saw an elderly gentleman with sparse white hair wearing a solemn frown and a navy blue cardigan. She had assumed that he needed the food more than she did, so she had just left it there. A short while later, still hungry, she had crawled wearily back into bed, and the next time she awoke the plate was gone. If she had stopped to think, at the time, she probably would have rationalized that the old man couldn't have just appeared and disappeared like that, and maybe she wouldn't have been so willing to give up the only meal she could recall in days. Anyway, it was lunchtime now, that is what the young man had said, and she certainly wasn't going to go without another meal.

Suzanne sat on the edge of her bed for several minutes waiting in anticipation for someone to bring her plate before she realized that the door was still slightly ajar. He had left her door open! She walked cautiously to the cracked opening and peered out. She saw a large, circular counter that took up the entire central area of the room. She could also see several televised monitors on the far side of the room. Suzanne wondered briefly if they were watching her as she watched them. There were at least five people behind the counter wearing the usual medical garb sorting through files, talking on phones, and engrossed in their work. However, she was not a fool enough to believe that they were so preoccupied that she could somehow slip past them unnoticed.

Suzanne plastered on her best smile and then brazenly opened the door the rest of the way. She walked out of her room and approached the formidable counter, fully expecting to be jumped, shackled, and returned unceremoniously to her cell at any moment. Because of this, she was completely surprised by the warm smile that greeted her once she arrived at this den of activity.

"Hello, Suzanne. It's great to see you up and around," a short, plain, blonde woman gushed. "What can I help you with?"

Suzanne was unsure how to take this apparent kindness. In fact, she was completely taken aback by this lady who seemed to be so familiar with her when she, as far she could remember, had never seen this woman in the entirety of her life. But Suzanne had nothing to lose. To still be standing outside the dank, miserable room that had held her captive for days was a small blessing.

"Um," Suzanne began shyly, "I was expecting someone to bring my lunch. I guess maybe they have forgotten."

If this woman thought there was something strange or unusual about her inquiry, there was no indication of it in the softness of her answer. Her smile remained gentle and genuine. "You'll have to get your own plate, dear. You will find it up there on that round table in the far corner of the room over there."

Suzanne lifted her eyes to look in the direction the kind lady had motioned. The mauve carpeted room seemed to go on forever, large and expansive, with colorful, cushioned chairs lining its perimeter. There was a huge grouping of overstuffed leather couches in the central area of the room. At the far end, in front of a massive picture window, she could see a large assembly of circular tables that were surrounded by comfortable looking chairs.

Other patients who appeared to be enjoying each other's company already occupied many of the tables. Suzanne tried to hide her amused grin as she realized all of the patients had one thing in common: they all had stocking clad feet. On her most creative days, Suzanne would have been hard pressed to come up with a way to use her shoes to harm herself, or anyone else for that matter, but they were obviously considered a lethal weapon.

Returning her focus back to the sweet lady in front of her, Suzanne asked, "You mean we don't have to stay in our rooms?"

"No, Sweetie, you don't. In fact, we actually prefer that you spend more time out in the day rooms."

Suzanne wasn't sure where or what defined these "day rooms," but the only thing that mattered was that she actually felt a sense of freedom again. Oh, there were still boundaries that couldn't be crossed, but like a bird that had been set free from a small wire coop into an expansive aviary, she mentally stretched out her arms and embraced her newfound independence, and the smile that started inside moved quickly to her face.

She sat by herself as she ate the well-rounded meal of a fried pork chop, some sort of greens which she couldn't identify, candied yams, cornbread, and a small piece of chocolate cake that was smothered with strawberries and whipped cream.

Suzanne, having been born and raised in Wisconsin, had still not become accustomed to the Southern style of cooking. For the most part, it was all just a little too greasy for her taste, and no matter how often she had tried to eat these things they called "greens," she never failed to grimace at the bitter taste they left in her mouth, and today was no exception. However, she was ravenous and could tell by the way the oversized T-shirt and her faded jeans were hanging on her that she had lost a considerable amount of weight. She needed to eat!

She could feel the other patients' curious eyes upon her and she knew they were probably wondering why she was there. Maybe it was wrong of her to be so antisocial, but she wasn't ready to talk to anyone, not just yet. For now, she was content to sit quietly on the sidelines and observe. Fragments of their dialog drifted in her direction and Suzanne began to realize that there was a whole lot about this place that she didn't know.

A very large woman wearing a bad wig at the table adjacent to her own was excited that her mother would be there to visit that evening. Suzanne could also hear another young, very depressed looking woman discussing a conversation she had just had with her boyfriend on the phone. Both confirmed for Suzanne that there was actually communication with the outside world. However, if that was true, why hadn't she heard from Kent? There must be some mistake! Surely, if she were able to receive phone calls, she would have heard from him by now. Oh boy. Did she really want to go down this road? Probably not, but she had already started. Why turn back now?

The truth was Suzanne didn't know what to think anymore or what to expect from her husband. After all, things hadn't been exactly "normal" with her the week before she had come to the hospital. She had known that Kent was aware something was wrong with her. She could see it in his worried frown and in the wrinkles that creased his handsome brow.

Kent had commented often that she didn't seem to be getting enough sleep, but he never questioned her when he arrived home to find nothing had been fixed for supper and it seemed she had become oblivious to the fact that she had two children that need-ed to be fed and taken care of. Suzanne wasn't exactly sure what had ultimately convinced Kent that she was no longer in control. Maybe it was her insistence that her father was about to die of a heart attack, his friend Art was going to die in a head-on collision, and someone else they knew was going to die of cancer. Didn't he understand? Everyone was dying!

However, Suzanne was experiencing life, dozens of lives, being born again and again, each time into a different life where she would only see a few highlights before she would experience her death in that life and then be born again into a new life.

Speaking of births, probably her insistence that she was pregnant even though Kent had a vasectomy and her tubes had been tied probably hadn't helped her in any way, but she could swear that she felt the baby moving inside of her. Whatever Suzanne's culminating act of lunacy was, Kent probably felt like he had no other choice but to admit her to this place.

She had been slightly distracted from the visions she was seeing in the blank screen of their TV as he got up from his recliner and went into their bedroom. He had closed the door behind him, something he had never done in the past. A short time later, she could hear the hushed tones of his voice and she assumed he was on the phone with someone. Once again, Suzanne had become intrigued by the images she was observing on their TV. It didn't matter that the set was turned off; the pictures she saw of herself experiencing different moments with her family were crystal clear on the screen.

When Kent finally returned to the living room, he told her gently but firmly that he was going to take her to see someone who could understand what she was going through. He had escorted her to the car and then taken her on that fateful ride that ultimately ended there, where she was. From that point on, there had only been silence from him. Would he want to see her? She wasn't sure. Had he tried to call? If he had, Suzanne didn't know or couldn't remember.

"Stop it, just stop," she heard another voice say, "Have a little faith. It will all work out."

Suzanne shook her head slightly as if by doing so she could

silence the voice. She got up from the table and carried her now empty plate to the cart where she had watched the other patients place theirs. For the most part, everyone had dispersed from the tables and went to comfortable areas to relax. Looking around her newly expanded surroundings, Suzanne suddenly became acutely aware that it still was not big enough. She continued to feel like she had nowhere to run or to hide. In her heart, she knew that regardless of how much freedom she was given or how expansive her world became, there was still no escape from those two heavy chains that entwined her very soul and held her captive: intense pain and insanity.

A small, ironic laugh welled up within her. If they only knew what was going on inside of her head, they would really think she was nuts! Thankfully, God had blessed her with a creative mind, and she had been able to cover some of the worst of her symptoms. If she hadn't lost control and let the others take over, no one may have ever known that there was even a problem. "Spacey" was her nickname, and most had just attributed her absent-mindedness to innocent daydreaming. Little did they know, when she didn't appear to be all there, she was actually fighting an inner battle. She was struggling to regain control.

Suzanne had made her way back to the observation area with hopes of getting some help to fill in her many blanks. She spotted the friendly lady who had assisted her earlier and beckoned her with a wave of her hand. "Would you mind answering some questions for me?" she asked politely.

"Of course not. How can I help you?"

"Well, I overheard someone say that there were visiting hours this evening. Is this true? And do you know if my family will be visiting?"

"Yes, the visiting hour is from six o'clock to seven o'clock. You are allowed to have four family members during that time. I am sure your husband will be here along with your two children. Kent has called to check on you quite often. He also completed the mandatory course that we require family members to take before they are allowed visitation privileges. I am confident that he and the children will be here for you."

"That's great!" Suzanne didn't even try to hide her enthusiastic smile.

The nurse's reply had been like soothing aloe to a soul that burned for any sense of normalcy. Just the idea of being able to see her children and her husband again thrilled her and filled her spirit with hope.

"Is there anything else I can help you with, Suzanne?"

"Oh, yes, just one more thing and then I'll let you get back to work, I promise," Suzanne said with an apologetic grin. "I noticed a shower in my bathroom, but there was no soap, shampoo, or the other necessary items needed to bathe," Suzanne continued as she indicated her disheveled appearance with a sweep of her hand. "I'm sure that I look awful. I don't think I have combed my hair or brushed my teeth in days, and there's really no telling how long I have worn these same clothes."

It wasn't necessary for Suzanne to continue. With an understanding look, the lady turned away and began methodically opening a cupboard and a drawer from which she withdrew a familiar looking makeup bag along with an overnight bag. Both pieces of luggage had the name Suzanne C. written in large black print across a piece of tape that was attached to their bulging sides. She handed the bags to Suzanne while explaining that they needed to be returned as soon as she was through with them. Fresh towels would be found in a closet down the hall, the lady continued to explain, and the laundry room, where she could wash all of her dirty clothes, was directly across from that. Well, maybe things were not as bad as they originally appeared, Suzanne surmised as she returned to her room.

She couldn't wait to discover what great treasures these bags held. While sitting on her bed and unpacking each item, she realized that she had taken simple things like her toothbrush for granted. She was delighted to see the bristled wonder there amongst other things that would bring her hygiene back to an acceptable level, such as a hairbrush, deodorant, and toothpaste. She even discovered a rose-colored lipstick to be used in the event that she decided to go all-out.

The overnight bag contained three different pairs of jeans and several T-shirts, a much-needed nightgown, and the flimsy under things she was accustomed to wearing. Tucked in the folds was the best surprise yet, a pale blue envelope with her husband's handwriting scrawled across it that held a card, which immediately brought a delighted smile to Suzanne's face. On front of the card was the picture of a sad, dejected looking puppy along with the words "I miss you! They say out of sight is out of mind..." As Susan opened the card, her grin grew even bigger as she continued to read, "And they are absolutely right! You're out of my sight and I am going out of my mind!"

The card was a typical example of her husband's humor and it seemed that he never failed to find a way to make her feel like he was right there with her, experiencing her joy or her pain, whatever it happened to be in that moment. The flowers he had drawn on the inside of the card were juvenile at best, but her heart overflowed with love as she read the scribbled words underneath. "Here are some flowers for you, darling. I hope they haven't wilted by the time you get them. All my love, Kent."

Suzanne questioned how she could have any doubt about Kent's unconditional love for her, but a part of her still wondered. He had seen her as he had never seen her before. He had seen her insanity up close and personal. How could he possibly feel the same about her? One thing was certain, Kent would be there to visit that evening and she needed to make things look normal and presentable on the outside even though inside she was still struggling to regain control and make sense of everything that had happened in the past few days.

She gathered her shampoo, soap, washcloth, and the skimpy

towel provided by the hospital and proceeded to the shower. As the warm water trickled down the aching muscles of her back, Suzanne recalled her conversations with Dr. Polland earlier in the day and smiled at the diagnosis the doctor had just seemed to pull out of thin air. She wondered if what she was experiencing was really bipolar manic depression. Well, she wouldn't argue with the depression part. Ever since the pain that seemed to torture every fiber of her body had gotten the best of her and taken away the one thing that she had always held sacred, her ability to work, she had admittedly been fighting depression.

All of her life, work was all she had ever known. It was the only thing of value she had taken away from her childhood. She had been raised on a large dairy farm in rural Wisconsin and had always worked from before sunup to long after sundown. She had carried this work ethic with her into her adult life as well, sometimes working two or three jobs at one time, not because she needed to do so to survive but because that was all she knew. Suzanne defined herself by her work. She was a waitress, a pharmacy technician, a store manager, a business owner, and more. Whatever her occupation at the time, that was who she was. However, when she was no longer able to work, she was at a loss as to how to define herself. She was nobody! So yes, it was depressing to be a 32-year-old nobody who felt like life was over because of crippling, constant pain that made it impossible to perform even the simplest of tasks, let alone hold a job.

She found the bipolar part very amusing. Maybe the doctor had seen some of the "others" and described them as highs and lows, but Suzanne was not about to volunteer any information on that subject because it was one facet of her life that she had no desire for anyone to examine. "Suzanne, how many times have we told you that we are here to help you? We don't know why you continually try to hide and look at us in such a negative light. There was a time when you were grateful we were there for you. Some of us are very offended!" That unmistakable voice came from the one Suzanne had come to consider a spokesperson for the others.

She reached for her towel and began drying as she tried not to respond to the voice. Why argue with something or someone who anyone else would tell her was just a figment of her imagination? In fact, she was sure that they were the reason she was in this place to begin with. She had been in so much pain and too tired to resist, so they had taken control, each contributing to the insanity those around her saw. It wasn't her. She wouldn't have done or said those things, so it was only logical to assume that she must be experiencing difficulties that required medical attention. Anyway, the shortest distance between where she was and her freedom was a road that did not include the twists and turns that would come along with revealing the "others," and she was certain of that.

"Look guys, no offense," she said silently, "but, I have got to get out of this place and that means I need full cooperation from all of you. If you are truly there to help, then you will allow me to take full control while you take a back seat, preferably a silent one as well."

There were some mumbled agreements and a few choice cuss words from one who always seemed to be very angry and telling Suzanne that she was being a complete ingrate, and then there was silence, blissful silence.

"Thanks so much!" Suzanne whispered quickly.

She had begun the tedious tasks of trying to disguise the darkened circles under her eyes, something that required her full attention, and she was grateful they had agreed to allow her this time of peace and quiet. Looking at herself in the mirror, once again she was dismayed by what she saw. She was so young, and some had even called her beautiful, but to her the pain was written all over face. Tiny lines seemed to appear out of nowhere, and the stripe of gray, which had been there since she was nineteen, in the front of her otherwise gorgeous mane seemed to be more pronounced than ever. In the past, she would have laughed and told those who mentioned it that this gray hair portrayed her great wisdom or that it was her lucky streak, but on this day she conceded that it just made her look old.

"Must we have this conversation again?" The gentle chiding in her heart came only from one source; it was God. "Must I tell you again how beautiful you are? Must I remind you that when you criticize yourself, you criticize me? I am the artist, the creator, and you could not be more perfect! There is perfection in all that you are."

Suzanne's smile was weak. "Thanks," she said, "of course, you are right."

"Of course!"

"As long as you are here, would you mind reassuring me that everything is going to be all right? As you can see, I'm in one melluva hess here, and it is hard for me to understand how any of this can be for my greater good!"

She knew God was still there because she could feel the warmth of love enveloping her soul like a hug, but the conversation had become one-sided again, unless you counted the gentle laughter she swore she heard at her attempt to avoid using the "H" word.

As Suzanne continued to dress and prepare for the evening ahead, she marveled at the change that had taken place in her relationship with God from her childhood to the present. It had taken Suzanne years to overcome the picture of the vengeful god she had been taught to fear from her earliest days. During her childhood years, she had rarely spoken to this god except to beg for forgiveness for her many sins. Somehow, the relationship had not seemed real or right to her. After all, if one thought about it, they would realize that it is totally impossible to have a relationship with someone you fear.

In her later teen years, Suzanne had concluded that there really was no pleasing this god. She felt that there was no way to live up to such high expectations, and so eternity in hell was a certainty for her. She had declared that if she must spend the rest of her forever in the torment of a fiery inferno, she would dedicate her life to pure enjoyment.

For the next several years, she had bounced from relationship to relationship, being promiscuous and fickle to the point that even she scared herself a little. In her defense, Suzanne declared that she had just been looking for love, but it was not to be found in any of the nightclubs she frequented or in the endless procession of one-night stands.

It seemed strange that Suzanne had spent so many years wandering blindly in the desert of her own ignorance when the love she had been searching for had always been there for her. How could she have overlooked the ultimate truth for so long? It was so simple! It was God whom she had been searching for all that time, for God is love--pure, unconditional, perfect love!

Along with that truth came even more truths that opened Suzanne's heart to a new and completely wonderful relationship with this God of love who looked in one's heart and not at their outward appearance. The days of fearing the wrath of God because she had cut her hair or found comfort in a pair of jeans rather than a dress were over. The legalistic god that her religion had created was a fading memory to her. Why had they limited the love of God and made it conditional based on one's behavior? Why did they preach that God was no respecter of persons in one breath and then proceed to tell this long story about the "chosen ones?" Why would anyone believe that God was a racist? Who was this fickle and unpredictable God they talked about that stretched out his arms and said, "Come!" in one moment and "Depart from me!" in the next? What kind of a contradictory God would declare to Moses, "Thou shall not kill," and "Thou shall not steal," and then tell Joshua to go kill and plunder the entire city of Jericho? Wasn't God supposed to be the same yesterday, today, and forever? Moreover, was there any explanation for how a perfect God was capable of experiencing imperfect emotions such as anger and jealousy? Who would even want to know this God?

Suzanne knew that somewhere amidst the contradictions and confusion there was some truth to be found. Her favorite of all truths was that perfect love castes out all fear. God is love! God is perfect love! There was no longer an impossible, fear-based relationship between her and God but one of immense awe and a love so great and so comfortable that she could never put it into words.

As Suzanne pulled her brush through the tangles in her hair, she smiled. She knew that she had only barely begun to understand God. How could someone like herself, who is so limited, even begin to fathom God? In her time and space existence, she really had no concept of the eternal. Living in a world full of limits and boundaries, it was very difficult to comprehend infinite possibilities. In a life where love had been doled out so rarely, it was very hard to imagine an unconditional and never-ending source. Suzanne stood for a few moments in silent reverence and let her heart express the gratitude she felt for this great being, and then she began to pray softly. "You know, God, I could really use a little help. Kent and the children will probably be here for a visit this evening and it would be terrific if they went home feeling like everything was going to be all right with me. You know how bad I hate the fact that they had to see me in such a state of insanity. I still don't understand why all this happened, but I am sure that you can see the whole picture from where you are, and I'm trusting you to steer me safely through this storm. You know I can't do it without you! I love you!"

Suzanne was now completely prepared for the evening ahead. In fact, she looked exceptionally well, all things considered. After returning her bags to the counter, she decided she would walk around and explore the limits of her newly expanded world.

Her first discovery was a small kitchenette off to the left of the observation area. As she looked around, she saw a large bowl filled with assorted fruits sitting on the countertop next to an icemaker. Adjacent to the ice machine there were several large plastic bottles of caffeine-free soft drinks. In the corner, a refrigerator was well stocked with small cartons of milk and juices as well as individually wrapped sandwiches, which were all labeled according to their contents. Quite a selection, she observed, everything from ham and cheese to turkey, roast beef, and even the old faithful PB&J. The freezer held individual servings of ice cream and sherbet. Finally, in the cupboards, there was an assortment of cereal and chips. Suzanne would discover in the days that followed that the hospital made these snacks available because many of the medications she and other patients were on had the side effect of making one feel extremely hungry. However, in that moment, she was just grateful to know that she wouldn't necessarily have to eat the food delivered by the cafeteria.

Adjoining the kitchenette was a large room decorated tastefully in shades of aqua-blue and green. This room also held some wonderful discoveries. There were puzzles, games, and books stacked in no particular order on shelves that covered an entire wall. On the far side of the room, there was a large, comfortable seating area with a big-screen TV as its focal point. As her eyes continued to travel around the room, Suzanne spotted an old upright piano sitting unobtrusively in the corner. Looking at it, she had a brief moment of regret that she had not done better during the few piano lessons she had taken as a child. It would have been nice to fill the quietness of the large room with the melodious sound of music.

Suzanne turned and was about leave the room when she spotted a dark-haired man who appeared to be in his early forties sitting quietly by himself at a small table by one of the windows. He looked so lonely and depressed, and although she could not think of anything to say to him, she felt compelled to go to him. Suzanne approached the table with a gentle smile and said, "Hello" in one of her friendliest voices.

He looked up at her, but his expression did not change. "Hi," he replied and then turned away to look with a blank expression out the window again.

This man obviously did not intend to invite her company, but Suzanne felt that for some reason she needed to stay. She pulled out a chair from the table so that she could sit facing him and then continued to make small talk.

"My name is Suzanne. I guess you could say I am new here. I just arrived a couple of days ago. What about you?"

"I must have gotten here a few days before you did, I remember you coming in. You seem different somehow," he said quietly.

"Well, it was probably pretty hard to miss someone running around naked, screaming that the building was going to explode, and then getting hauled, kicking and yelling, back to their room by three orderlies." Suzanne tried to make light of one of the scattered recollections she had of her insanity. "In my defense, I hadn't slept for a while before they brought me here, so I probably seemed to be a little crazy to a lot of people. The doctor said that sometimes lack of sleep causes a chemical imbalance in the brain and then leads to psychotic behavior. Anyway, I think I slept for the first two days that I was here, so maybe I am caught up on my Z's and things are back to normal again," Suzanne said with a wry grin.

"I wish things could be back to normal for me," he said wistfully.

He was looking down at his hands as he talked to her, and Suzanne's eyes were drawn in that direction. She was horrified by what she saw! Across the back of each wrist was a long, angry wound that had been stitched back together with some hideous black thread. She reached out and gently touched his hand and questioned him softly as to what had brought him to that place.

He shrugged despondently. "My wife. She found someone else. She wanted a divorce. I guess I just couldn't handle it." His voice trailed off for a moment, almost as if he was reliving the entire experience once again.

A few minutes later, it seemed he had found the strength to continue. The story he told was a sad one filled with intense hurt and betrayal. He expressed to Suzanne that life didn't seem to matter anymore.

Suzanne listened quietly, doing her best to let him know she cared. When it was obvious by the tears in his eyes that he had no desire to go on, she asked him calmly for his name, to which he replied, "John, it's John."

"John, I am going to tell you something that you may already know, but I want to remind you. God loves you! I mean, God really loves you! There is nothing that you, I, or anyone else could possibly do to make God stop loving us. When all else and everyone else fail us, God will never let us down. God is there for us always and in all ways. I have listened to your pain and I know it runs deep, but with each day that you remember and hold onto that pain, you relive that same hell and you rob yourself of experiencing the joy in that day. I know you have heard the saying, 'Let go and let God.' Well, that is what you need to try to do. I promise you, God has nothing better to do than pick us up when we fall, comfort us when we are in pain, cheer us on when we triumph, and love us with an unconditional love. I don't know, I guess I just assumed you believed in God. Forgive me if I have been too presumptuous," Suzanne ended with an apologetic smile.

"Actually, I do believe in God, and right now I believe in angels," John said quietly. "I am sure you were heaven sent. I really needed to hear what you just said. You have helped me out a lot."

Their conversation continued for some time as Suzanne tried to help John remember the things in his life that were worth living for and to encourage him to try to look past the pain into a more positive direction.

As other patients began to fill the room with an expectant air, Suzanne realized that it was nearing time for that evening's visiting hour to begin. She smiled politely at John and excused herself after reassuring him that if he ever needed to talk again, she would be more than happy to listen.

While walking away, Suzanne wondered briefly if maybe she wasn't in this place for herself at all and then dismissed the thought as quickly as it had come. She still didn't think of herself as highly as God did, of that she was certain. Every day she attempted to overcome the inferiority complex that had been instilled by her father. She still felt so unlovable, so totally imperfect in every area of her life, and no matter how often God reminded her that to criticize oneself was equivalent to finding fault with the Creator, she continued to do just that.

Suzanne approached the large picture-framed window at the front of the room where she had eaten earlier in the day and joined several other patients as they looked out into the parking lot that was visible just beyond a well-manicured lawn. It was obvious that they were all hoping for the first glimpse of their loved ones as they drove up. Suzanne was feeling extreme excitement at the prospect of seeing the children and her husband for the first time in what seemed to be weeks. She smoothed her hair with her hand and then looked down quickly at the clothes she was wearing. She looked okay, she assured herself. Everything would be just fine.

Suzanne could feel her heart begin to race as she spotted the familiar, gray Grand Marquis pulling into the parking area. They were there! She watched lovingly as the children jumped out of the car. Tyler was first. Her precious little boy was not so little anymore. He was only eight, but because of his size, he was constantly being mistaken for much older. He stood over five feet tall and wore a men's size nine shoe. She caught her breath and then laughed softly as she watched him trip over an untied shoelace. She was always telling Tyler to tie his shoes.

Little Nicole was never one to follow. She raced into the lead as they both hurried for the door. Nicole was a picture of beauty in her frilly pink dress, but Mom knew that underneath the softness of the dress there was a steel determination that she would have her way or make everybody else miserable trying. Suzanne often saw herself in the little six-year-old. She knew in her heart that, if channeled into positive direction, the energy and determination Nicole exhibited would take her to unimagined heights.

Kent wasn't far behind and Suzanne could tell from the way he was gesturing to the children that he was trying to corral them and calm them down before they entered the building. He looked very drained. Suzanne was sure that she had probably been the cause of many worried days and sleepless nights. She longed for some way to make it all better.

As they disappeared through the entrance at the front of the building, Suzanne walked away from the window and over toward the door through which they would soon arrive. She couldn't wait to hold them again and tell them how much she loved them.

Soon, the door opened and a line of people wearing visitor passes began to pour through and greet the waiting recipients with warm hugs. Suzanne scanned the faces quickly looking for her own loved ones. Nicole had pushed her way through the crowd and was the first to throw her arms around her mother's waist. "I missed you mommy," she said sweetly.

"I missed you more," Suzanne told her daughter as she savored the warmth of her embrace.

By then, Tyler and Kent had arrived and she pulled them both into the circle of her arms. She was doing a great job of holding back the tears; there was no sense in them seeing her blubbering. Suzanne knew that she needed to present a strong and positive picture of herself. She knew they needed to see her sane. She kissed Tyler and Nicole affectionately on their respective cheeks, whispering that she loved them as she did so, and then she turned Kent. "Oh, Darling, I have missed you so much!"

"Ditto," he whispered softly as their lips met in a long, tender kiss that said things words could never say. Nothing had changed unless their love for each other had grown stronger and deeper through the difficulties.

They all moved toward a vacant table and sat down. Suzanne could tell that, like her, they were all very uncomfortable with her being there, and nobody seemed to know quite what to say. After an awkward silence, Kent reached for her hand and whispered, "I'm glad to see you're back. You had me a little scared."

Suzanne smiled at him and tried to reassure him that she was indeed "back" as she intertwined her fingers with his. For the next hour, they spoke of what the children were doing in school, how things were going with his job, and all of the other usual things that filled their conversations before she had come to this place. If it wasn't for their surroundings, one might have thought things were completely normal.

Nicole, who always wanted to be front and center, had to sing her abbreviated version of "North to Alaska" for mommy. Suzanne's encouraging smile turned into giggles of hysteria as she tried to scold her husband. "No way, Kent! You did not teach my child one of your Johnny Horton songs!"

"Oh, you would be amazed at all the pearls of wisdom I have shared with her on our drive to school every day. I have even gotten her to talk like me too. The other day I told her to be careful closing the door so that she didn't slam her fingers in it and she looked up at me and said, 'Because that would really smart, huh?.' I laughed so hard. I didn't realize she was such a sponge."

"Yeah, a stupid sponge," Tyler said sarcastically as he poked at Nicole.

Trying to avoid a public squabble that was sure to break out if things continued in the direction they were going, Kent immediately got Tyler's attention. "Hey, tell your mother what you want to be for Halloween."

The kids took turns interrupting each other as they tried outdo the others idea for a costume. How they ever came up with a vampire cat-in-the-hat would always be a mystery.

Much too soon, the hour passed. An announcement over the P.A. informed all visitors that it was time to leave. The children had been showing signs of boredom, and although they were anxious to leave, they protested having to go home without their mommy.

"I'll be home sooner than you know," Suzanne assured them. "I'm already completely better now. I just have to persuade the doctor to let me come home."

That seemed to pacify the children, but Kent was not so easily convinced. "Darling, promise me that you'll take care of yourself and do everything the doctor says."

"I promise," Suzanne mumbled as she reached up and stole one last passionate kiss. "You know, I really miss you! I mean, I miss every delectable, edible inch of you. I am going to have to get the doctor to spring me from this joint so that I can come home and take care of you properly." She teasingly nibbled on his neck before she let him go.

Kent smiled at her and winked. "You better be careful, Honey Bunny, or you are going to get us both into trouble!" Reluctantly, he pulled away from her and called the kids together. After a few more parting hugs and kisses, they made their exit. Suzanne stood there for a moment holding back the tears and watching as they disappeared through the door and down the long corridor that would lead them out to the main entrance. She knew that it would be days before they would be allowed another visit, and she was already missing them more than parched fields thirst for rain.

CHAPTER FOUR

The days that followed went by very slowly for Suzanne. The doctor had determined that she was doing well enough to warrant being promoted from close observation to a room without the invasive cameras. This also meant that she would be allowed more freedoms, such as being able to leave the unit to go to the cafeteria and on walks outside. With the change in rooms also came the requirement that she would attend informative classes designed to help the patients adjust positively to the affects of newly prescribed medications and, in most cases, the diagnosis of mental illness.

The days became very structured and routine, and for Suzanne this meant boredom in its purest form. Breakfast was at seven o'clock each morning and then it was time for medication at eight o'clock. At nine o'clock, a walk was scheduled that allowed everyone to get out in the open and take in some fresh air. The rest of the day was just as organized. There was a meeting with her doctor around nine-thirty, and, an hour later, classes were scheduled until it was time for lunch at twelve-thirty. After lunch, more medicine and then a small reprieve before the beginning of another set of classes that lasted into the late afternoon. Supper was at five-thirty each evening, and afterward she was finally free to do as she pleased within the confines of the hospital unit.

Suzanne treasured those quiet evening hours. Hearing and seeing the difficulties of other, throughout the day as they each related their stories during group meetings pulled at her heartstrings. However, she felt helpless to do anything other than say a prayer for them. It was certainly becoming crystal clear that her problems were tiny in comparison to most, and she had a lot to be thankful for.

Suzanne spent most of her time at her desk writing in the journal provided by the hospital. She had always loved to write; it seemed to soothe her like nothing else. It was almost as if she was letting the part of herself that was beautiful and pure flow free. In the process, she washed away some the darkness and hurt within her. She also believed that by writing down her wishes and dreams, somehow it would bring them a little bit closer to becoming reality, so she wrote and prayed.

The things Suzanne wished for most in life were the priceless things that could not be bought with financial wealth. What she craved more than anything were simple pleasures, pure joy, unconditional love, to be enveloped by beauty, peace and harmony, and to be endowed with health, but not just for her; she wanted these gifts for everyone. Oh, how she longed for the world to be filled to overflowing with these precious treasures. However, if she could only choose one, she knew it would be love--perfect, never-ending, unconditional love. When all is said and done, love seemed to be the answer to every important question. Who is God? God is love. What would bring an end to all the wars and violence? Love, because through the eyes of love we would see a father, a son, a brother, a daughter, or a mother instead of an enemy, all with the same hopes, dreams, and fears that we have. What would feed the hungry and clothe the poor? Love. It is love that will move us to make the necessary sacrifices. What will heal this planet and bring it back to health? Love in motion. What are we all longing and searching for? Love! The truth was so simple, so very elementary, that even the smallest child could understand;

yet it seemed like so few were actually getting it. Suzanne knew that sometimes even she didn't get it.

She sat there at the small desk wondering to God, "If love is the answer to all things, then I suppose it is the answer to why I am here. So, am I here to learn to love and care for myself better, or am I here to spread a little love and sunshine to others?"

In her heart, the answer was immediate, "Both!"

Suzanne stiffly unfolded herself from the hard chair that she had sat upon for almost an hour as she wrote and talked with God. The pain in her back was reaching a crescendo and she knew she needed to walk to alleviate some of the aching stiffness in her knees.

She decided to check on Mary, the lady in a room just few doors down the hall. Suzanne shuddered as she remembered Mary recounting the story of the car crash that had taken the life of her only son and left her with a back injury that ultimately led to her addiction to prescription drugs. Mary was barely able to walk, and Suzanne's heart always went out to her as she watched her shuffle along in slow, baby-like steps to her different destinations. Suzanne had missed her at the evening meal.

The door was slightly ajar and as Suzanne knocked it opened even further. She could see Mary lying on the bed in the dim light of her room. The white covers were pulled tightly up around her chin, highlighting her rose-colored complexion and beautifully rounded cheeks. Her long brown and silver hair was pulled back in a single braid and her dark, deep set eyes, which had been staring up at the ceiling, slowly turned toward the door. "Come in," she said slowly and barely audible.

"Hi, it's me, Suzanne. I missed you in the dining room and I was just wondering if there was something I could do for you. Perhaps I could bring you a snack?"

There was a long pause and then Mary began to speak slowly. "No, I don't need anything. I just hurt so badly. I couldn't get up. I really appreciate your checking on me."

"I'm sorry if I bothered you," replied Suzanne, "I was just concerned about you. I said a little prayer for you earlier. I know things have to seem very difficult for you right now. I just want you to know that I am here for you if you need anything."

"Thank you. I'll be all right."

"If you're sure," Suzanne paused and then turned away from Mary's room feeling another wave of helplessness descend upon her.

She knew that if she had her way there would be no pain, no suffering, no bad, no disease, no death, no... She stopped herself. She had already learned that lesson too. Without the perception of down, there would be no up. Without bad, there could be no reference for good. Without the illusion of death, there would be no appreciation of life, so the real choice was to have neither or to have both. Adam and Eve chose to "know" or experience both. The funny thing was that in truth none of those things really did exist. The proverbial fruit from the "tree of the knowledge of good and evil" was not an apple but rather a hefty dose of perception and judgment, and upon its ingestion it created intense fear (the polar opposite of love), making this world full of dualities very real to us.

Suzanne had returned to her room by now and stretched out on her bed as she recalled the illuminating moment when this truth was made so clear to her. She had been trying to reconcile her past, to justify in some way the horrific actions of her father, when the realization had hit home. He did not perceive his actions as dreadful. He did not see himself as wrong; in his eyes, he was right and he was doing all the right things for all the right reasons. What she saw as abuse, he saw as his God-given responsibility to train her up in the way she should go. What she saw as anger, he saw as love; after all, if you love a child, you beat them with a rod and save their souls from Hell. How could they both look at the same thing and see it so differently? Perspective was the answer. They were both looking at the same thing but from two very different points of view. Suzanne was having a difficult time seeing through the blood and tears, and her father was having a hard time seeing around that big black book.

This realization had helped her understand much more. It seemed to her that humans, in general, go through life judging everything: what is good or bad, right or wrong, socially acceptable or downright rude and crude. There seemed to be a judgment about all things everywhere. This word is good, that word is offensive, this lifestyle is right, that lifestyle is sinful, this country is rich, and that is a third world nation. From religion to politics to parenting and social status, the judgments were never ending. Suzanne knew that if everyone would stop and look at things from another perspective, or if they took the time to experience and learn about something new, chances are they would once again change their minds about what was big or small, here or there, young or old, and right or wrong. She had learned that it was important to look through the eyes of others. A woman who sees a towering oak and says how large and majestic it is may have never stood next to a redwood. A man who climbs Mount Everest, looks down, and says, "You can see the world from up here," may have never been to the moon. How many times have we said this is the happiest or worst moment of our lives only to change our minds when we experience another moment of joy or sadness? Therefore, Suzanne believed the truth was that judgments are based on one's perspective, and our perspectives are formed based on our current knowledge and experiences. The interesting thing was that, the more one experiences, the less inclined they are to judge, for within the experience they are likely to find a place of understanding, common ground, and even forgiveness. In that place, some may even begin to understand that life is not about being right or wrong; life is for living.

Suzanne laughed at herself. Her mind never seemed to shut down; she was always looking for the answers to all of life's questions. She had been told all her life, "Seek and you will find." The answers she had found, however, didn't always fit in with popular opinion, so if she chose to expound to others the wisdom she had gleaned along the way, she most certainly would be labeled as "crazy" and no doubt be confined to a life in institutions similar to the one she now occupied.

Even now, as she lay there looking heavenward, her mind was filled with questions that she would love to ask the pope or some great theologian. For example, if the gift of God is eternal life, why is that we perceive our life to have begun when we arrived as babies on this earth when the true definition of eternal is to have no beginning or no end? Aren't we being cheated out of the "no beginning" part? However, that would bring up so many more questions. If we are eternal beings, where were we before we arrived on earth? Why boggle our minds with the thought that if the earth is God's footstool, then the entire universe that surrounds us must be something tiny to him like maybe the parlor of one of his many mansions. What is Gods idea of a mansion? Is it a building, or could it possibly be a universe or, better yet, billions of universes connected? Why put limits on God? There seemed to be a lot of limits placed on God. Evidently, according to some, the grace and patience of God had limits. The bi-polar god they created made no sense to Suzanne. How could they use words like love, grace, patient, just, and unchanging to describe God in one breath and in the next declare the same god to be an angry and jealous god who is ready to hurl us into eternal hell fire for lesser sins than the ones for which we imprison those we label as criminals? What egos we must have to believe we are big and bad enough to affect God in any way, let alone cause God, who is Love, to experience imperfect human emotions such as anger and jealousy! How silly we must be to believe that God, who knows every hair on our head, would one day change into some heartless being and say "Depart from me, I never knew you." What reason would God have to change?

Suzanne began to talk quietly to her heavenly Father. "I guess you know me well enough by now to know that I am not questioning you. What I am questioning is religions interpretation or perception of you, and even my own, because I am sure that it is imperfect at best. I am trying very hard not to put limits on you and to grasp the true meaning of 'with God all things are possible.' Please continue to help me to see those around me through your eyes. Help me to love perfectly and without judgment and never forget that there is a purpose to everything under the heavens.

"Oh yeah, one more thing. It's time for me to go home, and maybe you wouldn't mind letting Dr. Polland know! In the meantime, I really appreciate you watching over my family and giving them a little extra TLC. Thank you!" With that, she turned over and drifted into a dreamless sleep.

The following day started out with the usual routine Suzanne had become accustomed to during the week and a half that she had been hospitalized. Breakfast offered its usual array of scrambled eggs, slightly cold bacon, and a slice of toast that she washed down unceremoniously with a large glass of orange juice.

Suzanne returned to her room in the few minutes she had before the morning walk to tidy up, and there was a knock on her door. The doctor was making her rounds a little earlier than usual. Suzanne hurriedly finished making her bed and then sat down on the edge of it as the doctor took her seat on the only available chair in the room.

"How are you doing today, Suzanne?" the doctor questioned.

"A better question would be how are you doing today, Dr. Polland?" Suzanne replied with a smile. "I was really hoping you would be in a very good mood today and feel like signing the necessary papers to release me. I have been doing extremely well, as I am sure you are aware, and I really feel the need to be at home with my children."

Dr. Polland smiled. "You do seem to be improving daily. We just need to make sure that you are getting the proper dosages of medication at this point, but I see no reason why you won't be able to go home tomorrow."

If the doctor said anything else, Suzanne didn't hear her. Her mind, heart, and every part of her had already begun to rejoice like a freed prisoner of war. *Yes, there is a God that really does answer prayers!*

The rest of that day, between classes, was spent saying good-byes and offering words of encouragement to those Suzanne had come to know during her short stay at the hospital. The happiness she felt within radiated in her smile. Although she knew that she would probably never see these people again, she longed to show them that, even in this world that was shut off and shamed by society, a sense of peace could be found. If one searched, they could even find joy amongst the sadness, laughter to erase the tears, and, more importantly, no matter what their state, they could find God. Suzanne had learned that even though we may not be aware, God is always there; sometimes we just play peek-a-boo.

CHAPTER FIVE

The months following Suzanne's release from the hospital were extremely difficult. Not only was everyone around her continually questioning whether she was all right now that they were aware of her "little problem," she also questioned herself. After all, if one thought about it, hearing voices that others didn't hear was probably a good indication that something wasn't quite right.

For the most part, Suzanne tried to laugh off the concerns of others, but in those quiet moments when no one else was there, she had to face her own fears and concerns. She did not understand what had happened to her and why. Her fragmented recollection of the week before she went into the hospital was very disturbing to her, but she had nowhere to go and no one to turn to for answers. She definitely didn't want to worry her loved ones anymore than she already had, and her faith in the psychologist she was now required to see on a weekly basis was limited at best.

Suzanne's days were spent hiding behind a cheerful mask that presented to the world a woman who had fully recovered. Her children were taken care of, the home was reasonably clean, the meals, for the most part, were hot and delicious, and she found wonderful ways to show her husband that he was the man of her dreams. However, behind the disguise and in those moments when she no longer had to perform for the rest of the world, there was a woman who wondered and questioned. Who am I, really? Are these people, these voices that I hear, me? Are they a part of me? Are they real? What is their origin?

On her own, Suzanne began a quiet search for the answers. She spent hours at the library and local bookstore hoping to find a book that would somehow describe her "symptoms" and perhaps even offer a practical way to overcome whatever it was. Her search only brought about more confusion. Books about the unquiet dead, lost souls who didn't realize they were dead and who somehow attached themselves to the living and affected their lives in strange ways, causing abnormal behaviors, pains, and addictions, seemed to become a real possibility. Perhaps that was her problem. Maybe she was possessed!

The thought of possession led Suzanne down a winding road of fear and uncertainty. After all, it was just a theory, a rather odd one, but in those moments, any explanation, no matter how ridiculous, seemed to be a better option than having no explanation at all. It was unthinkable for her to accept the fact that she was just plain nuts and leave it at that.

Her weekly visits to the psychologist became somewhat of a challenge. Suzanne desperately wanted to confide in this doctor, but her fear of being forced to return to the confines of the hospital was very real. In her quest for answers, she felt like the proverbial mouse running through a maze. She didn't quite know which direction to take and which roads would ultimately lead nowhere. If she seemed too daring, there might be a snare that would bring her to a screeching and painful halt and leave her trapped once again behind those daunting metal doors. In any case, she still wasn't sure whether she was looking for an escape from, an excuse for, or an answer to her insanity.

In the midst of the turmoil and bewilderment that was taking place within, she was oblivious to the harmony that was flowing in the world around her. However, like a child waking out of a dream-filled sleep, Suzanne slowly began to observe subtle things happening that could only be answers to her desperate, silent pleas for help from God. The first and most marked alteration in this new fabric that was being gently but deliberately manipulated into something unmistakably beautiful came about a month later when she entered her psychologists' office for her weekly visit.

Suzanne had not come voluntarily; she had not done anything willingly that day. The night before had been a restless one filled with excruciating pain that left her feeling exhausted and not at all able to handle even the simplest task. She had coaxed herself out of bed and into the shower with promises that the warm water would bring some welcome relief. However, even the invigorating massage from the water as it bounced and danced its way across the aching muscles of her back failed to soothe her. From that point on, things had gone decidedly downhill.

Suzanne hadn't bothered to put on any makeup; there was really no point. The pain had spilled over into a heedless stream of tears that flowed silently as she continued to prepare for the day ahead. She had scolded and insulted herself along the way hoping that the "reverse psychology trick" would somehow motivate her or make her stronger. However, regardless of how many times she told herself that she was just being a big weenie or that she needed to invite someone else to her pity party, Suzanne could not ignore the one thing that had brought her to this place: stabbing, blinding, tormenting pain. So, that is how she arrived at her psychologist's office, walking slowly with a slight limp to favor the knee that was complaining a little more loudly than the other on that particular day and with her face proclaiming to the world that she had seen better days. Her eyes were slightly swollen, dirty tear streaks ran haphazardly down her cheeks, and there was that one tell-tale sign that she could never disguise whenever she had a good cry--a bright red nose that would give Rudolf a run for his place in history.

As Suzanne slowly lowered herself into the soft, comfortable chair covered tastefully in burgundy leather and designated for patients, she caught a glimpse of a woman sitting unobtrusively off to her right. Before she could question the presence of this woman, her psychologist began the introductions.

"Suzanne, I would like you to meet Dr. Joan Hawkins. If you have no objections, she will be sitting in on your session today. Helping patients like you who suffer from chronic pain is one of her specialties. As it turns out, I have been offered a new position out of state, and Dr. Hawkins will be replacing me within the next couple of weeks. I thought it would be wonderful for you to meet her today."

Suzanne gave a slight shrug. "It makes no difference to me." She was in too much discomfort to realize that she had been downright rude and that she had forgone the customary, "It's nice to meet you, Dr. Hawkins." In fact, she had barely afforded the woman a second glance.

"I'm delighted to meet you, Suzanne, and I am really looking forward to getting to know you better." Undaunted by Suzanne's lack of social graces, Dr. Hawkins was completely amiable.

Suzanne brought her gaze up from the little piece of white fuzz that she had been staring at so intently as it lay there against the background of the rich, plush, wine-colored carpet. She had been fascinated with how out of place it was in this office, which was decorated with such formal detailing. Like her, she felt it really wasn't meant to be in there, in that place, this piece of fluffy fuzz. Like her, it was probably questioning how in the hell it ever ended up in the company of two psychologists!

She looked directly at Dr. Hawkins. The soft waves of the doctor's coffee colored hair hung at shoulder length, delicately surrounding a face that was hard to read; she could have been 35 or 55, Suzanne couldn't tell. The doctor's golden brown eyes were just as intently studying Suzanne. The gentle smile on the doctor's face that reflected a delightful glimmer in the depths of her intent gaze surprised Suzanne. As the doctor continued to speak, there was even a hint of a smile in the lilt of her voice. It was as if she was challenging Suzanne to get beyond the pain and find a better and happier place to be in that moment.

"I have worked extensively with patients who suffer from chronic pain; in fact, I would venture to say it is my forte."

As Dr. Hawkins continued to list her credentials, Suzanne returned to her observation of this woman who was to be her new confidant and savior. She was so relaxed it even showed in her casual dress that would have been just as appropriate for a day at the mall. Suzanne liked that. She had come to hate the business suits donned by most doctors that declared, "Me: doctor. You: patient." She wanted to feel that she could confide in and relate to her doctor, but in the past she had found it difficult to get past the air of superiority that was even further emphasized by attire that seemed to make them unreachable. What Suzanne wasn't sure she could deal with was this positive, cheery attitude Dr. Hawkins seemed to have going on. Maybe it was meant to be contagious, but Suzanne just wanted someone to take her place, someone to understand her pain, someone to join her pity party and, yes, she wanted someone to realize that the torment she was suffering on a mental level was much greater than her physical distress, which was overwhelming.

Suzanne shifted in her chair in an attempt to relieve the stabbing pain in her lower and back and tried to refocus on what the doctor was saying.

"It looks as if you have seen better days." The doctor was decidedly blunt. "Would you like to talk about it?"

"What's to talk about?" Suzanne mumbled, "I'm a thirty-two-year-old woman who is faced with the reality that, on a physical level, my life is over. I am no longer able to work, or do anything else for that matter, without having to deal with indescribable pain, and now the one thing that I thought I had going for me, a halfway intelligent brain, has suddenly decided to malfunction on me as well. There is nothing left. There is nothing to talk about. If it wasn't for my children and my husband, there is no way I would be here! In fact, I am beginning to think I'm probably not even doing them any big favors by sticking around."

"So that's it? You're just going to give up? Your life is crap and there's no way it will ever be any better, so you're just going to throw in the towel? First of all, I don't believe you. The fact that you're here tells me that you still have hope, how ever little it might be."

Good grief, this woman was merciless. It seemed highly unlikely that Suzanne was going to get any sympathy from her. "All right," Suzanne said, decided to go along, "maybe there is a small side of me that believes I can overcome and conquer, but I've got to tell you, it is a very minuscule part of me. For the most part, I just see a future that looks very bleak. I mean, the reality is that everything that I have wrong with me is degenerative. It doesn't get any better than this. Do you have any idea what it feels like to look ten years down the road and realize that I may very well be in a wheelchair by then?"

The doctor's reply was simple. "So, don't look ten years down the road. Take one day at a time or even one minute at a time, if you need to. Concentrate on this day and the things you can do within this moment to improve your life and decrease your level of pain."

"Okay, doc, you tell me how I can do that! Go ahead, tell me how I can live in the now and take one day at a time! The only thing that gets me from moment to moment now are the lies I keep telling myself that the next minute, the next day, the next week will be better than this one! This day, this moment, is too painful for me! I don't want to live in this moment, I don't want to live in pain, and, more importantly, I don't want to live feeling like I am losing my mind!" The tears had returned to Suzanne's eyes and her voice, which had begun with indignant sarcasm, had faded away into a trembling whisper. "I don't want to live like this."

Dr. Hawkins' voice was soft but firm. "I recognize that you feel overwhelmed by the prospect of living in pain. I am aware that it can leave you depressed and feeling hopeless, but you need to understand that there are things both of us can do that will help you cope with your circumstances and make life a little more bearable for you. There are several things I would like to introduce into your therapy in the near future."

As Dr. Hawkins began to explain the things she had in mind to promote Suzanne to a more positive frame of mind, Suzanne once again became distracted by the gnawing pain at the base of her spine. She tried to move unobtrusively to a more comfortable position as she nodded understandingly at the medical mumble jumble spewing from this woman's mouth. Maybe there was hope. Maybe this doctor had some tricks up her sleeve that the others hadn't thought of. One thing was certain, on days like this; things really couldn't get too much worse. Suzanne had always been the type of person to try anything at least once, so she surmised it probably wouldn't hurt to cooperate with Dr. Hawkins, at least for a little while, and see if perhaps she really could help.

One other thing intrigued Suzanne as she listened; there was something about Dr. Hawkins that she really liked. What it was, Suzanne couldn't seem to put a finger on, but somehow she was beginning to feel like she had just met a kindred spirit.

The hour ran its course. As Suzanne rose stiffly from her chair to leave, she gave Dr. Hawkins a half-hearted smile and apologized for not being a little more delighted to see her there when she first arrived. "Hopefully, I'll do better next week," Suzanne said with a wry chuckle.

"I'm counting on it," Dr. Hawkins retorted with a smile.

The rest of the day proved uneventful for Suzanne. She returned home to take on what seemed to be her endless role of housekeeping. Suzanne had come to accept that her daily chores now took at least five times longer than usual because she was constantly having to stop in order to allow the pain, which coursed incessantly through every inch of her body, an opportunity to sub-side enough so that she could continue for yet another ten or fifteen minutes. She always felt like she was caught in a game of catch-up, never quite being able to accomplish all that needed to be done. Just once, she would love to be able to sit down, look around, and realize she had absolutely nothing to do. Perhaps it was a distant dream or some nebulous memory, but she still had a vague idea of just how good it must feel to be entirely done with all of her chores and still have daylight left.

Of course, if things had to be the way they were, she was cer-tainly thankful for the husband God had blessed her with; he never complained, not even a little. If something hadn't been completed or if things weren't quite up to par, he would quietly go about the tasks at hand. He was an expert at doing dishes, laundry, and even vacuuming. His cooking skills needed some improvement, but what he lacked in finesse he made up for in heart.

The mornings Kent made pancakes were her favorite. Those ordinary round pancakes would never do for the children. Oh, no, no, no. The surprises that arrived off the hot griddle were never ending. It was a production from beginning to end, but no one was allowed even a peek until the grand finale. Any attempt to find out what great works were in progress was kept at bay with the wave of the grand master's spatula. Then, one by one, his golden displays of art were brought to the table. Perhaps it would be a Mickey Mouse pancake for Tyler this time, and Nicole, well, she loved his horses even though they sometimes lost a leg or two. For Suzanne, the surprise was never what would arrive on her plate, it was only how big or how perfect it would be. Kent always brought her a heart and, in the process, never failed to win her heart all over again.

Suzanne had taken one of her many breaks to rest and recov-er when she was brought out of her musings by an unmistakable inner voice that was telling her, quite sternly, that she needed to get up and start working again. One look at the clock was all she needed to motivate her. The day was getting away rapidly. The children would soon be home from school, followed closely by her darling Kent returning from work. Supper was yet to be cooked, there were a couple of loads of laundry waiting to be done, and the floors still begged to be vacuumed.

Suzanne had planned a menu of scalloped potatoes and ham, accented with fresh steamed broccoli for supper. As she peeled and sliced the potatoes, she let her mind drift back to the voice she had heard earlier which demanded that she get up and go to work. She wondered what Dr. Hawkins would make of that voice. How would she explain the source of that voice? More importantly, Suzanne wondered if she would ever get up the nerve to share this deep, haunting secret with Dr. Hawkins. After all, how could the doctor ever help her if she was never introduced to the source of Suzanne's problem? However, Suzanne was not about to confide in anyone until she was positive that they had her best interest at heart and she was certain that they were not going to lock her up in that horrible hospital again.

With a generous sprinkling of cheese, Suzanne deftly finished the preparation of the scalloped potatoes with ham and slid it into the preheated oven. Straightening up, she looked despondently at the floor and realized that she would have to put off the vacuuming for yet another day. It would take all that she had in her just to fold another load of clothes, and at that moment, laundry took priority. The dirty clothes hampers had been full to capacity and clean socks were in short supply.

Suzanne was sitting in the middle of her bed surrounded by a mountain of warm, freshly laundered clothing she had just pulled from the dryer when the children came bursting through the door almost simultaneously. It was obvious by their heavy breathing that they had been racing from the bus stop. Nicole had won; she always did. Suzanne had a quick flashback to her own childhood. She had loved to run. Her father had told her once that she reminded him of a gazelle because of her long legs and how swiftly she ran. It was the only compliment she could ever remember her father paying her, and it had meant the world to her.

"How was your day today?" Suzanne called out from the bedroom.

"Fine," Nicole said without much conviction.

Suzanne could hear the refrigerator door opening and knew that there were more important things on Nicole's mind. She smiled as she got up from the bed and started toward the kitchen. She knew she was going to have to run interference or neither one of the children would eat supper that evening. "Okay guys, I know you're hungry but supper is going to be ready in less than half an hour. I don't want you to spoil your appetite with a bunch of junk."

"But, Mo-om," both children whined in unison, "We're hungry now."

"Yeah, Ma, we haven't had anything to eat all day," Tyler continued.

"I am sure you're right. Nothing but breakfast and lunch and the snack you took with you this morning. I can see you're starving to death." Suzanne teasingly poked at the pudgy softness of her son's tummy and then gently removed the large bag of potato chips from his grasp.

"But, Mo-o-om," Tyler protested.

"There are bananas and apples in the basket on the table. If you're really that hungry, you can eat one of them, and then you need to get right on your homework. I promise you, supper is almost done. You'll be fine," Suzanne said firmly.

Tyler responded with a "humph" and then grudgingly picked up his backpack and turned toward his room. He was not about to eat anything that was remotely good for him. No way! Fruits and vegetables were taboo as far as he was concerned. Suzanne knew that the teaspoon full of broccoli she would place on his plate during supper that evening would go untouched until it turned cold and her coaxing and pleading finally turned to threats of broccoli everyday for a week if he didn't eat at least one bite; that usually worked.

Suzanne was of the belief people could acquire a taste for any food if it was introduced often enough into their diets. In her heart, she hoped she was right about that, and for the health of her children, she wanted it to happen sooner rather than later. Of course, if they took after their mother, it might be a while. Just the thought of all those teaspoons full of "greens" she had tried in attempt to "acquire a taste for them" made her shudder with distaste. Yuck, yuck, yuck! Well, at least she wasn't plugging her nose before she put them into her mouth anymore, which in itself was a marked improvement.

Nicole had settled for a banana and started talking through a mushy mouthful about her adventures at school. "There was a boy in my class who told me he liked me today."

"Oh, yeah?" Suzanne turned away from the stove where she had been preparing to steam the broccoli. "Well, I guess that's not surprising since you're so pretty and so very likable."

"Yeah, I told him I might like him too, except I was already involved with someone else," Nicole replied nonchalantly, as if things like that happened every day.

"Someone else, hm? Well, who's the lucky boy?"

"It's just another boy. His name is Jared. He sits next to me in my class."

"So, you're involved with Jared, hm? Gee, that sounds pretty important! What exactly does that mean?" Suzanne was laughing inside at the way Nicole had said she was "involved" with someone else, but she managed to hide her amusement behind an interested smile.

"You know, Mom," Nicole said impatiently, "Jared said he liked me first. He said he liked me when we were in Kindergarten."

"Oh, yes, of course! I'm sorry for being so silly," Suzanne replied as she ruffled Nicole's hair. "Do you have a lot of homework tonight?" She decided it might be best to change the subject; just the idea of Nicole talking about boys at such an early age scared her a little. *God help us when she becomes a teenager*, Suzanne thought with a shudder.

"Nah, just a math sheet."

"Okay, well, you need to get started on it. Let me know if you need any help."

The front door opened heralding the arrival of the man of the house. "Hi, Honey Bunny, I'm home!" Kent's greeting was typically cheerful. "Mmm, something smells delicious," he commented as he reached down to reciprocate Nicole's hug. "How's it going, squirt?" he asked.

"All right," she replied in a carefree way and then skipped off to her room.

Suzanne was next in line. "It's just scalloped potatoes and ham, nothing fancy," she told him between tiny, tender kisses. "Mmm, you taste delicious! Maybe I'll have you for supper instead," she teased him gently. "I wouldn't have to worry about counting calories that way."

"You don't have to worry about counting them anyway, darling. You're beautiful! Not that I am trying to dissuade you from making a smorgasbord out of me. I mean, you know what I say when it comes to things like that; too much just ain't enough," he told her suggestively as they continued their embrace.

"Whew, it's getting a little steamy in here! It must be the broccoli boiling out of control. I can't imagine what else it would be," Suzanne replied innocently as she pulled away, remembering that she did need to tend to things in the kitchen. "Don't forget where we were. It's my move and we're both winning!" She laughed playfully and blew him a kiss over her shoulder as she returned to the kitchen.

"No chance of that happening," he replied as he passed her on his way into the bedroom to change out of his work clothes into a comfortable pair of shorts. He emphasized his remark with a little love pat on her bottom and then disappeared into their master suite.

Suzanne took care of the finishing preparations to the food and then smiled as she slowly set the table. It just kept getting better. Who would have ever believed a honeymoon could go on this long? It seemed like she and Kent would never tire of one another. They never argued about anything, ever, and their love-making was as frequent and as passionate as it had been from the very beginning, maybe more so. She loved being in his arms and feeling the warmth of his strong embrace. What amazed her most was how much she missed him when they were apart, even if it was only for the few hours he was at work. It was as if she was missing a part of herself. Her heart had become entwined with his. She had never felt like this about anyone before, she had never loved like this before, and it felt so absolutely wonderful to have that love reciprocated in such an unconditional way. How could one be more blessed?

"What are you thinking about so intently?" Kent asked as he came up behind her and kissed her on the neck.

"You. How much I love you," she replied quietly.

"I love you too, Honey Bunny," he said softly. "Do you need any help setting the table?"

"No, it looks like I've just about got it. I need to get the kids to wash up, and then I guess we can all sit down to eat," she replied as she scrutinized the table. She was trying to determine if she had overlooked anything.

"I'll get the kids. You sit down. It looks like you've done enough work for one day; you need to relax a little." There was a note of concern in Kent's voice as he pulled out her chair. "Come on now, sit," he ordered gently.

"Okay. All right," she retorted as she slowly lowered herself into the awaiting chair. "There, I'm sitting. Are you happy now?" Suzanne smiled up at him just in time to catch another kiss smack dab in the middle of her forehead.

"Of course, you know it doesn't take much to make me

happy."

Tyler arrived at the table with his nose already wrinkled in distaste. "I hate broccoli," he declared, as though it was some important news flash.

"Really? Well, son, I would have never known that if you hadn't just shared it with me. Thank you." Suzanne smiled at him as she placed two small broccoli florets on his plate. "The thing is, you've just got to try this broccoli. It is new and improved, guaranteed to excite the taste buds, and rumor has it that it now tastes a little bit like pizza!"

"Mo-o-om," Tyler whined in protest. "Do I have to?"

"The sooner the better. Once it gets cold, that new and improved flavor just, poof, disappears," Suzanne said firmly, knowing that the broccoli showdown had officially begun.

After a quick blessing, everyone enjoyed the simple fare as each, in turn, recounted the highlights of their day. Tyler was excited that his best friend, Josh, had invited him to go roller-skating and to spend the night that Friday. Of course, Suzanne told Tyler that would be fine, but only if he ate his broccoli. She loved it when she had that kind of advantage!

After some failed attempts at negotiation, Tyler conceded and then winced with disgust as he grabbed for his glass to wash down any small reminders that mom had won yet another round. "Yuck! It doesn't taste anything like pizza, Mom! I still hate it too!"

"I can see by that funny look on your face that you still aren't very impressed, but hopefully one day that will change," Suzanne replied with a gentle smile. "You need to learn to eat some vegetables, Sweetie."

The meal ended without any more theatrics, and then the children both disappeared outdoors to play with their respective friends. Kent retired to the living room to catch up on the local news. After a quick clean up in the kitchen, Suzanne decided that she needed to return to the bedroom to finish folding the clothes she had abandoned earlier.

As she walked through the door into the master suite, she was caught by surprise to find that all the clothes had already been folded and put into neat piles. There was also a marked absence of Kent's clothes. He could never seem to figure out where Suzanne's and the children's clothes went, so he only put away his own. However, he always did the folding part just right. Suzanne tried to hide her delight as she turned toward the living room. "Someone has been folding clothes on our bed," she said in a deep, gruff, bear-like voice.

"Oh yeah?" Kent replied with a twinkle in his eyes.

"Yeah, and they must have worn yours home 'cause they're not there anymore." By this time, she had plopped into his lap and was trying, unsuccessfully, to nibble on his neck between his shrugs and her giggles. She was finally able to find a vulnerable spot right at the base of his neck and, after planting a warm, wet kiss, she laughed long and hard. "Gotcha!"

"Look, you gave me goose bumps all over!" Kent said accusingly as if he was trying to scold her.

That just made Suzanne laugh a little harder, and then reality struck. "Oooh, oooh, ow, ow, ow, I've got to get up," she said with urgency in her voice. "Honey, help me up. I've got a hitch in my git-along."

Kent's amused smile turned to a look of concern as he gently pushed her to her feet and asked if he could go get her some medicine.

"No, I just think I need to lie down for a little while. It's been another one of those days." Suzanne knew that it wasn't necessary to elaborate. He had seen her pain, and she knew in her heart how helpless it made him feel not being able to somehow comfort her or make things better for her. It was times like this when she questioned why she was going through this and why the man she loved so deeply also had to share the burden.

Suzanne undressed and slipped into the silky softness of a red negligee as the words of her parents began playing like a scratched record in her head. "Suzanne, you need to examine your life. There must be something that you are doing that is not pleasing to God, because whom God loves He chastens."

In her heart, Suzanne knew that what she was experiencing was not a punishment; she knew God better than that. Looking at examples throughout the Bible, she felt it was clear that God was into "time-outs" and giving His children an opportunity to grow by reflecting on their past mistakes. Jonah was a pretty quick study with his 3 days in the belly of the whale. It took the children of Israel a smidge longer as they wandered through the desert, but the amazing thing was that eventually they all got where God wanted them to go. Suzanne knew that one day she too would arrive in that perfect place where God wanted her to be.

"You're already there."

"I am?" Suzanne questioned tentatively.

"Yes, wherever you choose to be in this moment, that is where I wish you to be."

"Wow! You never cease to amaze me! Yes, it is true that I did ask to be a stay-at-home mom, but maybe I should have been a little more specific. My health is important to me as well!"

Warmth, peace, love, joy, and other feelings Suzanne couldn't possibly put into words began to flood her entire being as she reflected on what she had just experienced. There was no other way to describe it. It was an experience. How could she possibly explain what it felt like to have an entire thought conveyed instantaneously in a way that was felt by all of her senses? Maybe it was a "knowing." Whatever it was, she didn't have the words to explain it except to say that it was like coming face to face with an eternal truth that no part of who she was could ever deny, and there was certainly no denying the source of that experience either--it was God.

Suzanne smiled lovingly. "You really do work in mysterious ways, don't you? All right, I'm going to trust you on this one."

It was some time later when Kent entered the bedroom and sat down carefully on the bed beside her. His hands were tender as he began massaging her feet and legs. "The kids are in the process of getting their baths. Is there anything else they need to do before their bedtime?" he asked gently.

"Is it that time already? Good grief!" Suzanne was amazed at how quickly the evening had passed. "Well, they both finished their homework before supper, so if their rooms are straightened up, I guess there isn't anything else I need them to do."

"All right, I just wanted to check." He paused for a moment. Then, while looking deep into her eyes, he asked, "How are you doing? I mean, really, are things any better?" Suzanne smiled up at him. "Of course, now that you're here." For now, that truth would have to do. There was no point in creating more worry lines on that handsome brow of his. She could tell by the concerned look in his soft, hazel eyes that he was not totally convinced.

"I hope so," he sighed as he got up to leave. "Let me go get the kids ready for bed and then I'll send them in to tell you goodnight. Are you sure there isn't anything I can do for you?" he questioned again.

"No, Darling, I'm fine. Really. No, wait! I just thought of something I needed!"

Kent's response was immediate. "What is it, Honey Bunny?" Suzanne smiled knowing that he would do his very best to fulfill her every wish; all she had to do was ask. "Well, what I need is pretty special," she suggested playfully, "I'm not sure you'll want to give it to me."

The teasing smile on Suzanne's face must have given her away. Kent laughed and returned to her side once more. He captured her soft lips with his. She reached up to pull him closer, and her lips parted to allow the passionate sweetness of their kiss to become even more intimate.

"Is this what you needed?" Kent whispered as he moved to nibble gently on her earlobe.

"Mmmm! How did you guess?"

Suzanne could tell Kent was reluctant to leave her, but their fun had been interrupted by the distinct sounds of an argument that seemed to be escalating between Tyler and Nicole, and it was obvious they needed a mediator. "I'll be back!" Kent's *Terminator* imitation brought a smile to Suzanne's face.

"I'll be counting on it," she replied with a wink.

The evening ended with the usual array of complaints as the children tried to extend their day. Nicole was still thirsty and needed to get yet another drink of water. Tyler had forgotten to put his homework in his backpack. They both needed to make one last visit to the restroom, and they had kissed mom and dad goodnight but they had forgotten the family dog, Jake.

With the children finally settled in for the night, Kent returned to the bedroom and stretched out on their queen-size bed next to Suzanne. He yawned lazily and then rolled over to wrap her in the warmth of his embrace. "How did things go with your doctor's visit today?" he asked quietly.

"All right. Oh, I forgot to tell you I'm going to be seeing a new psychologist. I met her today. Her name is Dr. Hawkins. She seems to be nice enough. I guess the doctor I have been seeing is supposed to be moving out of state or something, and Dr. Hawkins will be taking her place."

"Hm? Well, hopefully she'll be able to help you."

"Hopefully. Well, enough about me. How was your day?" Suzanne decided to turn the spotlight into a safer direction.

"Same old song, different verse."

Kent seemed bored with the route their conversation had taken and had found a vulnerable spot at the base of her neck with his firm, sensuous lips. As he nibbled his way up the side of Suzanne's neck, she caught her breath. The way his mustache was tickling her and the soft wetness of his kisses along her tender flesh was awakening a burning passion that only he could satisfy.

His hands were tender as he slid them under the satin negligee and cupped her breasts. He gently began to tease her nipples between his thumb and forefinger. The moan that escaped her lips was a mixture of pleasure and pain. She had never been able to find the courage to tell Kent just how excruciating the pain in her breasts was, one more area of her body that fibromyalgia had not left untouched. For him, she was willing to endure any amount of pain.

Being careful not to interrupt the mood of the moment, she rolled toward him and pressed her body against his, entwining their legs and capturing his lips with hers. His strong hand moved naturally along the curve of her back, massaging it as he moved down toward her buttocks. Kent stopped to give her ass a playful squeeze and then pulled her even closer. Suzanne could feel the hardness of his manhood as it stretched his black running shorts to new limits, creating the only barrier between them and ecstasy. She deftly pulled his shorts down and out of the way, her lips never leaving his as their kisses became more intense. "Yum, you really know how to turn a woman on," she whispered hotly against his mouth as her hand moved to pleasure him.

"Are you sure?" he questioned playfully. "Let me see if I can do better."

His mouth left hers and began burning a passionate trail that rapidly moved south of the equator. Suzanne wiggled and squirmed, muffling her moans of ecstasy with the corner of her pillow.

"Now you're in trouble," Suzanne whispered, "You've unleashed the wild thing in me!" With a quick maneuver, she was the one in the driver's seat and their bodies melded together in a frenzy of desire fueled by intense passion and love.

Later, when they were laying exhausted in each other arms, she dared to share with him just a small portion of her earlier revelation. She chose her words carefully, knowing that she could not reveal all. To do so would only promote worry and concern that she may be "losing it" again. "I just had a thought as I was lying here earlier. I realized that I am where I wanted to be; my prayer to be a stay-at-home mom has been answered. I know it seems like a painful solution, but it was answered just the same. The truth is; I would gladly endure the pain if that is what it takes for me to be here for my children. The thing that has me puzzled is why God chose to answer me this way. I mean, I envisioned us winning the lottery or something grand like that. I guess the lesson learned here is that, when we ask, we actually do receive, but it probably wouldn't hurt to be a little more specific. Something keeps telling me that there's another reason why I am where I am at this point in my life. It's probably one of those mysteries that only time can solve. For now, I guess I'll just try to be content and to have faith that somewhere, in all this mess, there is a treasure to be found. I have to keep reminding myself that God is looking at things from a different perspective than I am and is capable of seeing the whole picture during those times when I'm blundering around in the dark."

"Yeah, you've heard it said a thousand times: be careful what you ask for 'cause you just might get it." Kent sleepily kissed her on the cheek. "Goodnight, darling, I love you!"

"Sweet dreams. I love you too," Suzanne replied.

She watched as Kent punched his feather pillows into a comfortable nest to cushion his head and then roll over with his back to her. She lay there for a few moments lightly stroking his back with the tips of her fingers before she turned over and tried to relax into sleep.

CHAPTER SIX

Suzanne awakened the next morning trying desperately to understand the dream that had invaded her sleep during the night. It had been so vivid, so very real.

In the dream, it had been another era, some other lifetime, and although she and Dr. Hawkins appeared physically different, it was definitely them together in that tiny room. Suzanne could see everything so clearly, almost as if she were remotely viewing the entire scene and had access from every angle. It was like a movie set completely opened up to her, and she was a voyeur.

She and Dr. Hawkins sat side by side on hard, Shaker type chairs. The rough, large-planked wooden floor beneath their feet was strewn with straw. They both held string and some of that same golden straw and were tirelessly weaving it together to form a broom. There were no words spoken, but they smiled often. The love that flowed between, around, and through them ultimately became woven into every strand of the broom. It was a love much stronger than most people ever feel. Suzanne and Dr. Hawkins seemed to know they would need that love in some other place and time.

Suddenly, the scene changed. The room was empty except for the broom. There was a sense that the two women had died but the love they shared lived on.

Shortly, Dr. Hawkins joined Suzanne as she stood viewing a new home. Somehow, the broom they made had found its way into that home too. Instinctively, they joined hands as they watched a dark force enter the home. It was convinced that somewhere within this house there was a key to heaven. This destructive force was hungry for power and fed by fear. It tore through the home, leaving chaos in its wake, determined to extinguish any light and suck away any feeling of hope or joy. Finally, it stopped to tear the broom to shreds as it searched for the key. It screamed and shrieked, feeling that somehow it had been deceived.

Dr. Hawkins and Suzanne only smiled. They told the dark force that the key was still there and that when it found the key it would be free. They knew in their hearts that the key was love. That was how the dream ended.

Suzanne was never one to dismiss her dreams, especially not when they were that vivid. She had no doubt there had been a message in it for her. What was it? The explanation that seemed to nag at her, refusing to be quieted, was not one she was completely willing to acknowledge. After all, to accept that explanation would indicate that she believed in reincarnation, and that was something she wasn't sure about. It seemed impossible for her to believe that she and Dr. Hawkins had prepared to overcome, or sweep, the demons out of her life by weaving a bond of love so strong in another lifetime that they would connect in this life just for that purpose. What seemed more likely to Suzanne was that the dream was an indication that Dr. Hawkins truly would be there to help her overcome this force of darkness that she seemed to do battle with everyday, and she found comfort in that.

Suzanne pondered the fact that once again she was given the message that "Love is the key." She remembered distinctly the first time that message had been imparted to her. It was an experience she could never forget. Suzanne had been going through a stagnant period in her life and she seemed to be stalled as she waited for some direction from her divine source. One particular night, she suddenly found herself suspended in a quiet blackness, floating in the protection of what seemed to be a bubble. Everything around her was calm and peaceful, yet she was very agitated. It occurred to her that maybe the bubble was not protecting her at all. Rather, it may be containing any disturbance she may have caused in this place of serenity.

Feeling completely impatient, Suzanne had mentally began drumming her fingers because it appeared she was there "in spirit" and the physical act was impossible. It had been another one of those times when an entire thought had been conveyed to her instantaneously. "What are you waiting for?"

Somewhat taken aback that an all-knowing God was asking her what she was waiting for, she had snapped her reply. "You, I've been waiting on you!"

Immediately she could feel the warmth of God's unconditional and unbounded love enveloping her very soul. "The key is love. Love will move you forward. Fear will hold you back. Love changes everything, including your impatience. Add some love and it becomes anticipation. Love is the answer, love is the key."

It was an "Ah! Ha!" moment, the darkness was filled with a brilliant light, and she had been returned to her earthly life to reflect on this deep truth.

Suzanne was brought out of her musings by a shrill beep from the alarm clock. It was time to get the children up and ready for their school day. She moved stiffly and pushed herself up out of bed. Grimacing in pain, she shuffled toward the children's rooms, but there was no indication of pain in the little tune she sang as she approached their bedroom doors. "Come on, you lazy cowboys, rise and shine. Another day, a dollar's pay, and everything looks fine."

Nicole was the first to meet her mom in the hallway where she intercepted her with a lazy hug and a good morning kiss. "Morning, Mom."

"Good morning to you too, Sunshine! Let's see how fast you can get ready for school." After giving Nicole a gentle nudge toward the bathroom to get her started, Suzanne proceeded down the hallway toward Tyler's room.

"Come on, Tyler. Let's see those feet hit the floor." Tyler responded by pulling his comforter even further over his head in an attempt to ignore his mother's prodding. "Getty-up, getty-up, getty-up, let's go!" Suzanne began tickling her son through his covers as she continued to insist that he open his eyes to a new day.

Realizing that mom wasn't going to settle for anything less than seeing his baby blues wide open, Tyler finally began to stir. Sitting up, he began rubbing his eyes. "Turn the light off, Mom. It hurts my eyes," he protested.

"They'll adjust. You need to get moving." Suzanne kissed him quickly on the forehead. "Come on now, you don't have much time."

Twenty minutes later, the children were rushing out the door with Suzanne yelling after them. "Have a good day. I love you. Be good on the bus. Good luck on your spelling test."

Turning back from the front door, she spotted the family Cockerpoo eyeing her from the couch. "I don't know about you, Jake, but I am going back to bed." She patted him on his soft, curly head and then limped back toward the bedroom. "My body is protesting a little too loudly this morning."

Jake was not far behind. After sticking his butt in the air and stretching his front paws all the way out, he rose to all fours and lazily followed her to the bedroom. Without any hesitation, he found a comfortable spot at the foot of the bed, curled up, and settled in for a morning nap.

Looking at the rumpled bed, Suzanne realized that she hadn't even remembered hearing Kent leave for work that morning. He never seemed to mind that she was usually in the midst of her deepest sleep right when he awakened to start his day. In fact, he always laughed and found great amusement in the way that Suzanne puckered up in her sleep to kiss him goodbye as she mumbled an incoherent "I love you." Since the sleepless days and nights that had landed her in the hospital, she felt Kent took comfort in seeing her in the state of slumber. He worried constantly that she was not getting enough rest. She knew he was probably aware that it was usually way into the wee hours of the morning before exhaustion and a liberal dosage of medicine were finally able to overcome her discomfort enough to allow her to catch a few winks.

Suzanne snuggled down into the cushiony nest of comforters and pillows that she had piled around her hoping to find that spot where her biting pain would collide with the downy softness of her surroundings and create the perfect atmosphere for oblivion. It must have worked.

Suzanne was startled out of a dreamless sleep by the thump of Jake jumping off the foot of the bed and onto the floor. At the same moment, she was aware that she was not alone. She could hear slow, deliberate footsteps approaching her bedroom door. Her mind began to race. *Who would have entered the house without knocking? How late was it anyway? Who could this be? Maybe it was Kent. Was he sick? Did he come home early from work?* Perhaps it was her mother. On the rare occasions that her mother visited, she had been known to come in without knocking, but she usually called out to let Suzanne know she was there. Whoever this was, they were not speaking and they were headed straight for the bedroom! While her mind bounced from option to option, Suzanne became aware that she was paralyzed. By fear? Maybe. She didn't know, but she was completely unable to move or speak. All she could do was lay there and observe.

Out of the corner of her eye, she saw an elderly hand reach out to pat Jake. He had met the intruder in the hallway just outside of her bedroom door. The fact that Jake's bobbed tail was visibly wagging and he was not barking indicated to Suzanne that this was not a stranger. It may have been her expectation to see a familiar face or the fact that she was extremely nearsighted, but either way Suzanne was completed deceived by her first impression of the elderly woman who entered the doorway to her bedroom. Initially, she had thought it was her mother. However, as the woman approached her bedside, she realized that it couldn't be her mother. There was no doubt that she bore a striking resemblance to her mother, but this woman was not her mother! Surprisingly, even though this stranger was directly beside her, Suzanne suddenly realized that she felt no fear. Still, she was unable to move or even speak. However, her other senses seemed to be heightened. She was distinctly aware of the cool, pungent fragrance of lilacs that wafted through the room upon the entrance of this gentle lady. The perfume seemed in perfect harmony with the lavender dress she wore which was scattered with a brilliant array of pastel flowers and accentuated by a lace collar. Her graying hair was drawn back in a simple bun, and the warm smile that generated from her pale blue eyes softened a face that was wrinkled and weatherworn. She never introduced herself. She merely picked up Suzanne's hand, which was laying there motionless on top of the comforter, and cupped it between her own two aged hands. Suzanne's eyes were drawn to those hands, so small, so dainty, so cool and soft, and yet the visible veins and age spots told a story of hands that had labored long and hard. She was about to return her focus to the face of this stranger when, suddenly, after quietly assuring Suzanne that everything was going to be all right, the gentle lady just disappeared.

Suzanne blinked hard and then sat up quickly in bed realizing in that instant she was no longer paralyzed. "What the heck?" she exclaimed, "Who in the world was that?"

The sound of her voice brought Jake running from the living room where he had settled in after leaving the bedroom. His soft brown eyes peeked out from beneath his curly black hair. The questioning look on his quirky canine face spoke volumes.

"You think I've lost my marbles, don't you Jake?" Suzanne asked defensively. Then, after giving it a moment's thought, she conceded, "You're probably right. That was just too weird to be real!"

Suzanne fell back onto her pillows and turned her focus in a heavenly direction. "Dear God," she began slowly, not quite knowing what to think or to say, "I'm not sure what just happened here, maybe it was a dream or my overactive imagination, and there's even a good possibility I'm just plain nuts, but it felt more real than that. You know me. I really do believe that with God all things are possible, so I'm not going to just dismiss this. I honestly needed to hear that everything is going to be all right. I guess you knew that, and if this is how you chose to tell me, I want to thank you. I have to admit that I have an inner peace now that I didn't have before. Somehow, I no longer doubt that everything really is going to be okay. Thank you! Um, I guess we're going to have to keep this one just between you and me for now. I have no desire to revisit Shady Grove! You know, just when I think I have you all figured out, you go and pull something like this on me! You are constantly surprising me! I like that. I like that a lot!" Suzanne paused for a moment. "Well, it's time to get up and start my day. I know I don't have to remind you of my usual requests, but it just makes me feel better to ask. Please, watch over those I love, surround them with your protection, love, and light, and provide for their needs. For myself, God, just give me the strength and courage to make it through my day and ease my pain. Help me to stay in a positive frame of mind.

Oh yeah, and if you can do anything to make all these stupid wars go away, that would probably make a lot of people happy. Just thought I'd mention that since you've got the whole world in your hands. OK, I'm signing off, hope you got all that."

Suzanne sat on the edge of her bed for a few minutes shaking her head in disbelief. At the same time, she was consciously aware of the light scent of lilacs still lingering in the air. The simple message that everything was going to be all right seemed to reverberate throughout her entire being and give her renewed strength and mental fortitude. That day was going to be a good day; she had no doubt.

Suzanne had many good days after that.

CHAPTER SEVEN

Suzanne stood in front of the calendar with mixed emotions while looking at the reminder scrawled in red ink. She had an appointment with Dr. Hawkins that day at ten o'clock. She went through the motions of preparing for her visit almost as if she was on autopilot. Her mind was on the dream she had had less than a week earlier in which the doctor and herself had overcome a dark force with love. Suzanne hoped so badly that there was truth in that dream. She prayed silently that somehow this doctor would be open minded enough to understand what she was going through without writing her off as a hopeless case of insanity. It would also be nice to have some explanation for those things she had experienced that weren't normal by any stretch of the imagination. Finding the courage to disclose all the things that kept in her in a state of confusion was going to be difficult, and Suzanne pleaded for strength to do so.

It was a twenty-minute drive from her home to the doctor's office and Suzanne realized that she was probably going to be a few minutes late. "Oh well," she shrugged to herself, "Shit happens."

Although she had already excused herself for lollygagging, at the last minute Suzanne decided that maybe the doctor wouldn't be as forgiving. There were eight cylinders under the hood of her car and the challenge to race with the clock proved to be incredibly enticing. She gave her full attention to skillfully weaving her way in and out of the city traffic, daring the stoplights to be anything but green and ignoring all posted speed limits.

"You're driving very dangerously, Suzanne! You're going to get us all killed! Why don't you let me drive? We may arrive a little late but at least we'll arrive in one piece!" There was no mistaking the firm tone in the voice Suzanne heard.

"Oh great! Just what I need," Suzanne retorted. "If I recall correctly, the last time you asked me to let you drive, you just kept on driving and driving, and I ended up in the loony bin! No thanks!"

Almost instantaneously, Suzanne seemed to flash back to that awful night when everything had gone so horribly wrong. It had been one of the longest twenty-four hours of her life. She had spent six of those hours in the waiting room of her orthopedic surgeon because he had been detained for several hours in emergency surgery, delaying all of his scheduled appointments. Suzanne had been there for her last follow up visit after having surgery in an attempt to center her left kneecap. The pain she was experiencing was excruciating, and it seemed to be focused in the area where two screws had been bored through the tendon that needed to be reattached to the bone in her lower leg. This pain combined with all the other discomfort she experienced on a daily basis had robbed her of sleep for over 96 hours. It was no wonder she had felt delirious and unable to function.

The doctor had even made a notation in her chart that evening stating that she seemed "unstable." It had probably been Suzanne's insistence that the screws were coming out and her tearful pleas for him to do something about it that had prompted the doctor to write this observation, but he did nothing to detain her. After telling Suzanne that the X-rays showed everything looking completely normal and reminding her to be careful not to fall because, should that happen, the damage may not be repairable, she had been sent on her way.

The walk to her car seemed to sap Suzanne of any remaining strength and she fell, overwhelmed by exhaustion, behind the wheel of her Mercury Grand Marquis. "God help me," she had cried. "How am I going to make it home?"

She gave in to the insistence of that very same voice she had just heard encouraging her to let him drive. She had remained conscious through the first couple of stoplights and then it was as if she had allowed herself to disappear into a fog.

Her next conscious memory was finding herself reading a road sign that indicated that she was not on her way home; instead, she was headed in the opposite direction on her way to New Orleans. She had gathered herself together enough to get the car turned around and headed back in the right direction. "You missed the exit," she accused indignantly, "I thought you said you could do this! I could have been home by now!"

Suzanne remembered turning off onto the exit that would get her back where she had started, but once again she lost consciousness before she even came to the stop sign at the end of the ramp at which point she needed to go north. Because she was drifting in and out of awareness, it wasn't until an hour later when Suzanne discovered that instead of heading north she was once again on her way south. This time, her apparent destination was Gulfport. She had struggled to regain control but had been unsuccessful. It was as if her body was no longer her own. She was vaguely aware of subtle changes that would occur to her as her car careened at alarming speeds down the empty stretch of freeway. Although it was her body sitting behind the wheel, it seemed to take on the appearance and mannerisms of whoever chose to drive. She observed herself going from a large, rugged man with an extremely heavy foot to a careless and carefree woman with long, straight hair. What an annoying habit she had, constantly flipping her hair back over her shoulder with a wave of her hand like that! When she became an elderly gentleman with labored breathing who also seemed to suffer from very poor eyesight, there was a few moments of consternation and then, once again, oblivion.

The night had turned into the early hours of the morning, and Suzanne volleyed between oblivion and vague awareness.

At one point, she had found herself on the beach strip in Gulfport, MS. Blinded by her tiredness and the glare of lights from the casinos and other businesses that thrived on 24-hour tourists; she was struggling to drive but unwilling to lose control again. It was then that she had heard the voice of her sister, Jean. Convinced that she was now able to telecommunicate with her sister, Suzanne had informed her of her distress and then became convinced that Jean was going to arrange for her to get a hotel room for the night. She had stopped at one of the many hotels along the busy strip and waited in the lobby for quite some time, checking frequently with the desk to see if her sister had taken care of the details so she could get a room. Finally, after being assured repeatedly by an irritated night clerk that Jean had not called to book a room for her, Suzanne had wearily gotten back behind the wheel of the car and headed north. City lights, darkness, oblivion, more lights, confusion, car lights, and darkness again, lights, another city (but which one?) on and on she drove.

Over seven hours later, she had been jolted back into reality. In the state she had been in, she had felt no pain, but in that instant there was no denying the agony within her body. Once again, she had screamed out in desperation, "God, help me!"

Almost instantaneously, a quiet calm enveloped her. "You'll know where you are in just a moment. It is very important that you drive now. You'll be able to get the rest that you need in just a few minutes. It is important to stay focused now. I am here with you." The words flowed through her in a relaxing wave and simultaneously the pain had subsided to a bearable frequency.

After rounding a sharp corner on a wooded, country road, she arrived at a stop sign. She peered through the early morning fog trying to determine which way to go when, suddenly, she recognized the old gas station in front of her and realized that she was only about five miles from her parents' home.

She had stumbled through her parents' door at 3:00 a.m. and told her mother that she needed an ambulance. But because she was walking upright and there were no signs of physical trauma, her mother had just helped her into the guest room.

"Mom, I need a pair of man's pajamas; it's important," Suzanne said weakly.

Too tired to argue with her daughter, her mother returned with a pair of her dad's cotton pajamas and then left the room to get some homeopathic medicine that she would later muscle test for Suzanne. Her parents had little or no faith in conventional medicine, so mom was doing what she would normally do during a medical crisis.

Suzanne struggled into her father's pajamas. She knew she had something important to do. She needed to speak for her brother, Steven. All those times when her father had tied him to water pipes and trees and then wailed on him unmercifully had to be set right. She drew on her brother's strength and she could feel his voice come through her. She entered her parent's bedroom and stood tall and unwavering at the foot of their bed. Her father roused and lifted his head up. "What's going on?" he demanded.

"You hurt me! Don't you understand? You really hurt me!" Suzanne's voice had taken on a deep, masculine tone and it boomed out loud as if being released from some pent up place.

Hearing what was going on in the bedroom, Suzanne's mother hurried in. "Something is wrong with her. I haven't figured out what's going on yet." She was quickly pushing Suzanne out of the bedroom door as she continued, "I am going to get her into bed and test her for some medicine. I'll take care of her."

After getting Suzanne back into the bed in the spare room and filling her mouth full of little white pills, her mother called Kent. "I think she's delusional," she told him.

Kent was relieved beyond words to finally discover where Suzanne was. It had been too soon to file a missing persons report, and he had spent the night pacing the floor, worried sick. After a lengthy conversation, he convinced her mother that Suzanne was probably just suffering from lack of sleep. "I haven't seen her sleep in almost a week. I don't know how she is even functioning at all. Please, just try to get her to rest and I will be there as soon as I can."

After he hung up, Kent quickly arranged for the children's care and then rapidly drove the sixty miles necessary to pick her up and bring her home.

It was probably a combination of Suzanne's insane ramblings on their way home and later, as they sat there in their living room, her insistence that she had a message from his deceased father, which had convinced him that her mother had been right, Suzanne was delusional and she needed help that he could not give her.

"No way!" Suzanne returned to the present. As she manipulated her away around yet another slowpoke, she reiterated, "No way in hell! There is no way I will ever, ever, as long as I live, allow you to take control again! I may be crazy but I am not stupid enough to fall for that again! Oh yeah, by the way, I intend to speak to Dr. Hawkins about you today. Maybe she has a plan for your eradication!" Reliving the horrors of that awful night had put Suzanne in a foul mood.

"There was a time when you were happy to let us take control. There was a time when you needed us and loved us, but I guess you have forgotten." There was sadness in the voice as it trailed off. Then, almost as an afterthought, he added, "We still love you and we'll always be here for you."

Suzanne tried to block out the voice as she pulled into the parking lot of the small, white office building. She had made it on time, but just barely.

A chime on door of the office alerted the receptionist to

her arrival. Looking up from her desk with a friendly smile, the young woman told Suzanne she would let Dr. Hawkins know she was there. "Just make yourself comfortable. She'll be with you shortly."

Moments later, Dr. Hawkins arrived to escort Suzanne back to her office. "How's it going today, Suzanne?" she questioned as they walked together down the hallway.

"Uh, fair, partly cloudy," Suzanne replied glumly.

Dr. Hawkins chuckled. "That's one way of putting it, I guess."

They were both seated comfortably within the sanctum of her office and it was obvious to Suzanne that Dr. Hawkins was ready to get down to the business of being a doctor. "Would you like to talk about it?"

Dr. Hawkins was doing what these doctors do best, asking questions. Suzanne decided she would need to ask a few questions of her own if she was going to find out just how much she could confide in this doctor. "Actually, I don't really want to talk about me right now. I just want to get your opinion on a few things. I want to know if you believe a person can be possessed, you know, by demons or maybe disembodied spirits or something like that," Suzanne asked tentatively.

The smile never left Dr. Hawkins' face. "Suzanne, what kind of horror movies have you been watching lately?" she teased gently.

"Horror movies aren't my style. It's just that I was reading this book about the unquiet dead and I was wondering what you thought about the idea of possession."

"It's obvious you're on an important fishing trip here, Suzanne. I actually know of the book you're referring to and yes, I have read it. I can tell you that I have a colleague who is also a friend of mine who believes very strongly that it is possible to be possessed and is trained in helping individuals release those negative energies that may be affecting their lives in adverse ways. Myself, I have not gone into the subject that deeply, but I think you will find that I am very open-minded when it comes to those gray areas where fact meets theory. So, do you think you're possessed?"

"No," Suzanne protested, maybe just a little too loudly. "No. On the other hand, maybe? I'm not sure. I guess I'm not sure of anything anymore. It's just that weird stuff happens to me that there really isn't any logical explanation for."

"Now you're going to have to tell me what you mean by weird. You've got to remember that in my profession I see a lot of weird. Weird could be any number of things. I've got one patient who is convinced he is in contact with aliens. Do you find that weird?" Dr. Hawkins queried.

"No, in fact, I don't. I actually believe in a God that didn't just start or stop creating in a seven-day period. I believe, quite strongly, that we are definitely not the only beings God decided to create. It is hard to know what capabilities other forms of life have, so, in my ignorance, I am not in any position to say that man is weird, a liar, or nuts. Maybe we are the ones who are out of touch with reality. Maybe it is our refusal to look and listen outside the bounds of what we consider to be normal and sane that is limiting our perception of what really is!" Suzanne ended her impassioned speech with a quick apology. "Oops, I guess I got a little carried away there. You probably would have settled for a simple no, hm?"

Dr. Hawkins was smiling at Suzanne as she assured her that she liked her honesty. "So, a man who has contact with aliens is not weird. Help me out here, Suzanne. What, for you, defines weird?"

"Okay, how about this. I love to write but there are times when I sit down to write and I know it is not me writing. The words on the paper are not mine and the handwriting is not mine; it is as if someone else is controlling my hand. Is that weird enough for you?" Suzanne watched carefully for Dr. Hawkins' reaction knowing that this was the moment of truth. She had believed in her dream, she had opened up to this woman, and now the ball was no longer in her court.

Dr. Hawkins showed no sign of alarm at her revelation. Instead, she seemed genuinely interested and encouraged Suzanne to demonstrate, if she could, by handing her a sheet of typing paper and a pen.

"Okay, I don't know what is going to happen here any more than you do, but I will start by writing something myself so that you can compare my style of handwriting with whatever else may be written later." Suzanne paused for a moment and then deliberately wrote a simple line across the top of paper. It said, "One day I will tell you about a very special dream." Suzanne stopped and handed the paper back to Dr. Hawkins. "This, Dr. Hawkins, is how I write, and the message I wrote was one I intended to write."

Dr. Hawkins took a moment to read the message and then with a quizzical look in Suzanne's direction she told her that she looked forward to hearing about the dream. She then handed the paper back to Suzanne and waited expectantly for her to continue.

Suzanne placed the pen upon the paper once more but this time it moved quickly in large sprawling cursive that was completely unlike the words Suzanne had just written so thoughtfully in a neat, careful row at top of the page. Suzanne watched as the message unfolded and was somewhat taken aback by what she read on the paper.

"I am a guide. I am here to help Suzanne without interfering in her free will. I am not of this earth. My purpose is to help direct Suzanne to a higher awareness. That is why I am here. That is why we are all here."

"Okay?" Suzanne's raised eyebrows and the fact that she probably sounded a little freaked out was all Dr. Hawkins needed.

"All right, Suzanne, I can see that you think that was weird. Would you care to share it with me?" Dr. Hawkins asked calmly.

"Um, not really, not just yet. First, tell me how you treat that guy who believes he communicates with aliens? I mean, have you locked him up and thrown away the key?"

"Of course not! He does very well in outpatient therapy and he takes medicine to help control the voices. Why are you so concerned about him?"

Suzanne slowly handed the paper toward Dr. Hawkins. "Maybe because I might have a few 'aliens' of my own, and the last thing I want is to be committed again." Her voice was firm in an attempt to convey to Dr. Hawkins that hospitalization was not an option.

Suzanne observed the expression on Dr. Hawkins face as she read what had been scrawled across the paper. *She's good,* Suzanne thought to herself. There was no glimmer of surprise or any other emotion for that matter; Dr. Hawkins was a regular poker face. Suzanne queried, "Alien or crazy person? What is the verdict?"

Dr. Hawkins finished scanning the message. After removing her reading glasses, she looked thoughtfully in Suzanne's direction. "So you were not the master of these words?" she asked, holding up the paper.

"Nope. Sorry. I can't take credit for them. It's kind of freaky, wouldn't you say? The thing is, that isn't everything. Just before I went to the hospital, I could literally feel other people taking turns using my body while they drove my car. Everything about me changed--my mannerisms, my breathing, my voice, everything! I was aware that it was happening, at times, but it was as if I was on the sidelines observing and then it seemed like I didn't exist at all. I disappeared into oblivion with no memory of anything for hours. Now, that is how I define weird!" Suzanne's brave front began to crumble and her chin quivered as tears began to roll down her cheeks. "The worst part is not knowing what to think. I just want some answers that make sense," Suzanne sobbed.

"Suzanne, I am not going to be able to give you those answers in this one hour timeframe. I have a lot of questions too, ones that you need to answer honestly for me so that I can try to determine exactly what we are dealing with here and how best to help you. If you'll give me your permission, I would also like to discuss your case with the other doctor I told you about earlier since it seems that you are expressing concerns about the possibility of possession. Is that okay with you?"

Suzanne nodded tearfully. "Yeah, I would appreciate it. I need all the help I can get."

"Okay. Now, is there any other 'weird stuff?' It is important that I have a complete picture if I am going to be able to help you."

"Just a few more things." Suzanne hesitated, somewhat reluctant to go into the darkened corners and pull out the skeletons that only she knew were there. "Sometimes I hear voices that I am sure no one else hears, and I've had visions of sorts where I see or experience certain things."

"That's all?" Dr. Hawkins asked with a smile in an attempt to lighten Suzanne's mood. "All right, let's start with the voices. Are they audible or in your head?"

"I experience them both ways."

Dr. Hawkins continued her line of questioning. "What do the voices say? Do they tell you to harm yourself? Is there more than one?"

Suzanne answered each question in turn. "The voices, for the most part, encouraged me, helped me, or calmed me, but there was one who seemed very angry. Yes, there is more than one. Yes, I can distinguish between them."

Dr. Hawkins didn't miss a beat as she scribbled notes on the yellow legal pad in front of her. "So, what is your explanation for all of this? Do you think you are psychic or something like that?"

"I really don't know," Suzanne replied in frustration. "That is why I am here. I thought you could figure this out for me. The visions I have are not always of this lifetime, and sometimes not even of this world, so there is no way I could prove that there is validity to anything I am seeing. In addition, I would have to believe in reincarnation to even accept some of the things I've seen and, frankly, I'm not sure I can. Am I psychic? I sincerely doubt it. I have had only one vision become reality and, I've got to tell you, I would rather it hadn't. It was when I was a teenager. I kept having a reoccurring dream about my friend, Michelle. I saw her getting killed in a car accident.

"One Sunday afternoon, around 5:00, I felt a sudden urge to go to my bedroom and write a poem. The poem I wrote was gruesome, not the usual, flowery love stuff I was used to writing, but it seemed to just flow out of me like it had to be written. I still remember every word.

THE ACCIDENT
Blood splattered.
Body battered.
Dreams shattered.
Gone, all that mattered.
Tears, remorse,
An endless source,
No recourse,
Death impacts with force.
Angel, fly.
Soar way up high.
Don't ask why.
It's time, goodbye.

"My parents didn't allow us to have a TV or radio, so I had no way of knowing, but when I got on the bus Monday morning and Michelle was not there, I knew in my heart what had happened. Later, my other friends confirmed that she had been in a car accident and, on Sunday around 5:00 in the afternoon, she had been removed from life support.

"For a long time afterwards, I felt so guilty. I believed that maybe I could have saved her life if I had just warned her. After an experience like that, I can assure you, I have no desire to be psychic. I quit writing after that too. I used to write all the time when I was younger, but after I wrote that poem, I just stopped. I don't think I wrote another word for years. It was only recently, since I haven't been able to work, that I started writing again."

"That might be something to consider," Dr. Hawkins commented as she glanced at her watch. "Our time is up for today, but I promise we will pick up right here next week. In the meantime, I want you to have my new pager number in case you need to get in touch with me before your next scheduled appointment. Try not to let yourself get caught up in trying to figure this out. Okay? I am here for you."

"Somehow, I could sense that you would be," Suzanne said with a knowing smile. "Thank you!"

CHAPTER EIGHT

It seemed almost silly, but Suzanne found herself looking forward with great anticipation to her next visit with Dr. Hawkins. In the short time Suzanne had spent with the doctor, she had been so completely at ease. For the first time in her life, Suzanne sensed that she had finally found someone with whom she could share those secrets she had hidden for so long. More importantly, she felt like there was finally a ray of hope breaking through the darkness. Suzanne had been very impressed by how open-minded the doctor seemed to be. There had been no judgment in Dr. Hawkins responses, and she appeared to display a genuine desire to help and understand Suzanne. Time would tell, of course, but there was no denying the inner feeling that God had come through once again. Suzanne viewed Dr. Hawkins as an answered prayer.

As the week progressed, Suzanne found herself thinking of Dr. Hawkins often and mentally replaying the dream in which the doctor and she had woven a bound of love in another lifetime. It might have been easier to write it off as just another silly dream if she could somehow explain the instantaneous bond she felt with Dr. Hawkins. How could she argue with her heart? What justification was there for this feeling of having known Dr. Hawkins all of her life or the comfort and complete trust Suzanne experienced in her presence? It was times like this when she was forced to question her belief that a person only gets one life, one chance, one blink in relationship to eternity to get it right with God. This concept hardly seemed to reflect the meaning of a just God of love and grace, but Suzanne had not given it much thought until that point. She had just blindly accepted the dogma taught by her parents and the church she had been raised in.

Never doubt that when one begins to seek with a willing heart and open mind, the answers to even the most difficult questions can be found. Suzanne had discovered that God was delight-fully fun to play hide-and-seek with. Once she had decided that she really did want to know, it was time for the game to begin. Suzanne presented the question in a simple prayer. "Dear God, it is my desire to know whether there is any truth to the theory of reincarnation. Help me to set aside all of my own thoughts and beliefs. Please, open my mind and prepare my heart to accept truth. As I search for the answer to this question, please guide my every step. Amen."

The "amen" had barely escaped her lips when suddenly Suzanne found herself remembering the words of her little daugh-ter, Nicole, as a child of two, barely able to speak. How strange to be recalling something that, at the time, seemed like the gib-berish of a small child. Suzanne could still remember the way her darling Nicole had climbed up into her lap and snuggled into her arms and then, out of the blue, she questioned, "Mommy, do you remember when I was your grandma and you used to sit on my lap like this?"

Suzanne had been puzzled especially since the one grandma in Nicole's life lived six hours away, at that point, and the only time Nicole had ever been introduced to grandma was the day of her birth. How did "grandma" find its way into this two-year-old's limited vocabulary?

In retrospect, Suzanne wondered why she had dismissed Nicole's question without even a second thought. Perhaps more disturbing was the fact that now the question had come back to haunt her and it refused to be ignored. "Mommy, remember when I was your grandma and you used to sit on my lap like this?" The question danced on and on to a song that refused to end, along with a simple statement, "A child shall lead thee."

Suzanne knew from previous experience that when she asked a question of God, the answer would be confirmed over and over again in a multitude of ways, so, in the end, the question no longer existed. In its place there was only knowing, so she waited expectantly.

In her search, she turned to the source from which she had been taught as a child, the Bible. It didn't surprise her that it had fallen open in her hands to the first chapter of Ecclesiastics. "That which has been is that which will be again...so, there is nothing new under the sun." Then there was the promise that Elijah would be sent "again" at the end of Malachi, a prophecy that was confirmed by Jesus when he declared that John the Baptist was indeed Elijah in Matthew 11. From that point on, Suzanne seemed to be inundated with even more proof that there was a reason to question her long held belief that this one life was all there was.

A television program that covered a story of a four-year-old child telling her mother that the bridge they were crossing was where she was killed "before" and that her mommy now hadn't been her mommy "then" once again brought Nicole's question to mind, "Remember when I was your grandma..." Suzanne began to question how it was possible for these children to recall such memories. Do we, as adults, tell the children that what they are saying is not real or right so often that they begin to believe us? When does the veil fall into place, that cloud that separates us from any remembrance of where we came from or who, or what, we were before we arrived on the face of this earth?

For every question Suzanne asked, there seemed to be even more information to sift through. As she probed into biblical history, she discovered that, at one point, there had been references to reincarnation in both the Old and New Testaments, but the Roman Emperor Constantine decided to delete the references to reincarnation in 325 A.D. His actions were confirmed by the Second Council of Constantinople in 553 A.D. because they felt that if people believed they had more than one life to seek salvation, then the church would not prosper. It never ceased to amaze Suzanne how often religion used fear tactics to enslave their parishioners. Fear was what they used to fill the church pews and, more importantly, the collection plates.

Suzanne began to realize that she would probably never have any tangible proof that a soul has more than one opportunity to experience life on this earth, or anywhere else for that matter. However, one thing was becoming abundantly clear. There was even less evidence to confirm the theory that the lifetime we are now experiencing is all we are allotted. In fact, if one truly believed that with God all things were possible, to even doubt the possibility would put limits on God. Suzanne knew that, like most, she too was guilty of confining God to a small box because she was always trying to fit Him into her clouded perception of time, space, and eternity. To try to fathom the greatness and boundlessness of God was mind-boggling. How could she begin to comprehend a God who in a matter of days created this magnificent mansion she knew as the universe around her? A mansion so expansive and so full of wonder that even if she were given a million lifetimes to explore it she could never fully begin to discover all the treasures it held. Suzanne knew that the Great Creator did not stop creating. God only rested for a day. What great palaces were prepared before this one or after God rested, and how many more universes were formed with God's awesome power? How could she wonder why God had given the gift of eternal life? There were so many places to explore, so much to learn, so many things to do and be, and so much to love and cherish. The gallery stretched on into infinity exhibiting the art of the Great Master, with each great room and each magnificent chamber open for our learning, our experiencing, our viewing, and our enjoyment, places prepared for us to experience and share.

Suzanne's quest for an answer had whiled away the days and weeks, and she still searched. But she was in no way prepared for what God had in store for the grand finale.

It was a typical morning. She had gone back to bed after seeing the children off for school. An hour or so later, Suzanne was aware of the sun streaming through the window as she rolled lazily out of bed. She was still rubbing the sleep from her eyes when she realized that something was terribly wrong. She had walked out of her bedroom and directly into a living room instead of the kitchen she was familiar with. As she scanned the room in front of her, a thought kept racing through her head. *This is my life, but it is not the one I'm consciously aware of. I need to get back. I need to get back!*

Suzanne took one last look around the living room. She was obviously in a mobile home. The dark paneling, avocado carpeting, and even the outdated television set and the Atari lying haphazardly in the floor indicated another era. Yet, strangely, Suzanne was aware that Tyler and Nicole had gone off to school and forgotten to put away their game center, so there it lay, waiting for mom (her) to put it back in its place under the television cabinet.

I need to get back! There was an unmistakable urgency now.

Suzanne turned around and stumbled across an ironing board leaning against the wall.

I need to go back, but how? How do I get back? She thought. *Maybe I should just go back to the bedroom.* As Suzanne made her way back toward the room she had awoken in, she screamed, "God help me!"

Suzanne had barely uttered her desperate plea when she found herself gasping for air back in her own familiar bed. "What in the world?" she exclaimed. "I don't get it! I just woke up in another life! It was my life, but it was not this life! Either I am going crazy again or you've got some explaining to do, God!"

"I created you in my image. See?"

"Oh! Okay? I get it! That was a pun!" Suzanne paused, somewhat perplexed. She knew that God had given her all that she needed, but she still wasn't sure she completely understood. And then, in a flash, it became as clear as a reflection in a mountain lake. Suzanne sat on the edge of her bed shaking her head, still unable to completely absorb what she now knew to be truth. There was only one, one life, an eternal life, and it is experienced in an endless array of ways and places all in the timelessness of one eternity. One is all. All is one. All is eternal.

As Suzanne got out of her bed and walked toward the closet, she stumbled across her ironing board. "Wow! A parallel reality? Déjà vu?" Whatever it was, she conceded, it was all possible.

CHAPTER NINE

As promised, Dr. Hawkins had consulted with her friend and fellow doctor regarding what therapy would be in Suzanne's best interest. They both agreed to use a more traditional approach to begin with, giving Dr. Hawkins the opportunity to become more familiar with Suzanne, who was a relatively new patient, and to allow Suzanne to eliminate the possibility of a more "acceptable" explanation for the things she was experiencing. Of course, taking the traditional approach meant that once again Suzanne would have to explain, in detail, what role she felt her father played in her life and how he affected who she was today.

Suzanne arrived at her scheduled appointment with Dr. Hawkins with a typed letter addressed to her father. It was only a copy of the original she had given to her father over a year earlier, but she felt that she needed to present the letter to Dr. Hawkins as a way of convincing her that she had long since forgiven her father. As far as Suzanne was concerned, it was a closed issue. She loved her father dearly. More importantly, she no longer gave him the power to hurt her. She had finally come to see the man who hid behind the mask that he wore. It was a disguise of control and a masquerade of perfection, but behind it all was a man consumed by fear. "I cannot be wrong!" he would always say, "I have to answer to God, so I must be right!"

The irony was that this overwhelming fear he had of being wrong and his need to micro-manage his world so that it would meet his definition of righteousness or perfection was actually controlling him. However, until he was ready to see that truth for himself, she could not help him; she could only love him unconditionally.

Suzanne handed the letter to Dr. Hawkins as she entered the office. "This is a copy of the letter I told you I had written to my father. Sadly, I don't think he understood it, but I felt like I needed to write it. So, whether it was for him or me, I am not sure. The bottom line is I have forgiven my father."

"Would you like me to read it now?" Dr. Hawkins questioned.

"Actually, yes I would. I need you to understand that my relationship with my father is no longer an issue for me," Suzanne replied.

Suzanne was silent as she watched Dr. Hawkins read the letter, but in her mind she could still see every word.

My Dearest Father,

Today I remembered who you are. I am so sorry that I had forgotten. From this day forward, I promise I shall always try to remember, for today is definitely a day of celebration. Today I remembered that we are all perfect, divine beings created by God. Like snowflakes, we all appear different, but we are perfect just the same, for God could not create anything other than perfection.

Throughout my life, I have perceived you to be less than perfect. I believed, as you had taught me, that only sinners would do bad things. However, I now understand that that we each have a different perception about what is good and what is bad and who is a sinner or a saint. And, for the most part, everyone tries to do what they believe to be good or right.

I clearly understand now that, when you beat me so furiously, you believed you were doing the right thing. You thought that if you beat me with a rod, you would save my soul from hell. From my

point of view, I was in hell and I thought you were so wrong to pun-
ish me so harshly. You see, what you believed to be for my good, I
could only see as bad. We both had a different judgment about the
same thing, and so it is with every part of our lives. You think sugar
is poison and I think it is absolutely wonderful. You love farming
and I would rather not. We go through our lives constantly judging
what is good or bad, right or wrong, fun or tedious; there seems to
be no end to our judgments. But, I realize now that everything that
exists just "is" and, regardless of how we perceive it, it continues
on being exactly what it has always been which is absolutely per-
fect. So, today I want to thank you for all the bruises, busted lips,
and all the blood I shed at your hands, for now I perceive that you
intended these things to be for my good. I understand now that,
within those moments that seemed so imperfect to me, there was
a Father who believed he was showing his love toward me.

I also want to thank you because, had it not been for all the
wrongs I believed you committed against me, I would have never
been able to experience forgiveness. Forgiveness is an incredible
thing. It is one of the most exhilarating and freeing emotions a
person can ever experience, but without something or someone to
forgive, one would go through life without ever experiencing the
wonderful beauty of forgiveness. So, thank you for each and every
blow. Thank you for every cruel word. Thank you for inflicting so
much pain. Thank you for giving me a reason to forgive.

One last thing, we are all self-"right"-us. Each of us believes
we are right and that we are doing only good things for all the right
reasons. This is our perception. But, it is very rare that anyone else
will ever see us in the same light as we see ourselves. Some see
what we believe to be our greatest strengths as our biggest weak-
nesses. For example, you feel that your determination to always
be right is a great attribute. Many around you see it as your great-
est flaw because you are never willing to admit your failings or
to say that you are sorry, and most have little respect a man who
cannot do this. So, who is right? Who is justified? Is it possible for

all to be right? Is it even more likely that we are all different with varied viewpoints based on our experiences and perceptions, so our judgments will also be different? Perhaps right and wrong are just matters of opinion that are as varied as the faces across time and in the end cease to matter. What remains, what is constant, is love.

So, here is the greatest truth, my dear Father. I love you as deeply as you love me. My love for you is as unconditional as God's love is for both of us and, in that love, that perfect love, we also are perfect. Sometimes we forget as I have done, and for that I am very sorry.

Now, for both of us, I release the pain that I have held for so long, believing you had given it to me, and in its place I accept all the love that I now know was your intention to give. Thank you for that love.

Your Daughter, Suzanne

Dr. Hawkins looked up as she finished reading the letter. "There is some pretty deep stuff here, Suzanne. You are probably right in believing that your father may not have completely understood."

Suzanne shrugged. "Maybe I shouldn't have given it to him. Maybe I wrote it for my own healing. But, you know what they say about hindsight being twenty-twenty! Anyway, a part of me still hopes that one day he will understand it all, and until then maybe he heard me say that I loved him."

"Let's hope so!" Dr. Hawkins replied. "I realize that you feel you have settled this issue with your father, so we are going to move on, but I am not willing to shut that door completely. There is still the possibility that a lot of the physical pain you are experiencing could be in some way related to suppressed emotional pain. This could be pain that you are consciously unaware of or unwilling to acknowledge."

"Of course, somehow I knew you were going to say that. You are the professional here, so I guess I need to trust your judgment. The truth is I don't feel that delving into my less than happy childhood is in any way helping me today. Maybe I am not being realistic about how all that then could be affecting me now, but at this moment I feel there are other things contributing to my insanity. I would really like to talk to your doctor friend. If nothing else, maybe she could ease the concerns I have about being possessed."

Dr. Hawkins seemed unabashed by Suzanne's straightforward delivery. "I can see that this is very important to you, so I am going to set up an appointment for you with her. Your insurance will probably not cover her fee, so you need to be prepared to pay that. Also, it is at least a two-hour drive. Are you sure you'll be able to make the trip?"

"I'll make it. If I have to leave four hours early and stop every 15 minutes, I promise you, I will make it!" Suzanne could barely hide her enthusiasm.

"Suzanne, I don't want to be a wet blanket here, but I feel like you are hoping that your visit to Dr. Mendenhall is going to solve all of your problems. I need you to understand that, while I expect that she will be able to help you, things like this take time. Your symptoms did not appear overnight, so it may seem unrealistic to think that someone could wave a magic wand and make you all better instantaneously."

"That's true, but I can always hope!" Suzanne interrupted with a smile.

"There is a lot to be said for hope! Okay, I'll set up the appointment and then give you a call in the next day or two with the details. Our time is about up for today. Do you feel that we are covering enough ground in these half-hour sessions?" Dr. Hawkins queried.

"Well, you know, if I had my way, I wouldn't come at all, so if you are asking me whether or not I want to return to our hour long sessions the answer is absolutely not. It is a good thing I like you just a little bit; it makes coming to see you somewhat bearable,"

Suzanne teased.

"Oh get out of here!" Dr. Hawkins bantered.

"With pleasure!" Suzanne was not to be outdone. She could hear Dr. Hawkins chuckling softly as she made her exit.

Suzanne's mind, heart, and hopes were all racing ahead to her encounter with Dr. Mendenhall. She had waited patiently for months wishing Dr. Hawkins would finally see things her way and allow this visit, and now it seemed she would soon be able to know if her self diagnosis was accurate.

Dr. Hawkins called a day later with instructions and directions. "Because you are going to have to travel quite a ways, and we are all aware of how difficult that will be for you, Dr. Mendenhall has cleared a two hour session for you next Wednesday. She suggested that you do a few things in preparation for your visit. You may want to write them down." Dr. Hawkins paused while she waited for Suzanne to get a pen and paper and then continued. "Dr. Mendenhall advised that you might want to consider wearing light colored clothing for awhile, white if possible. I've noticed that you almost always wear black, so this could be somewhat of a change for you. Also, she mentioned it is important to keep light around you. You can do this by burning candles. Dr. Mendenhall would also like you to visit a Catholic church where there is a Eucharist and other symbolic things like a crucifix. It is important that you are aware and note how you feel in the presence of these things. One last thing, relax!" Suzanne could hear the soft, reassuring smile in Dr. Hawkins voice.

"I'll try. Thanks again for setting this up for me. I really appreciate it!" Suzanne replied.

"No problem. Just be sure to keep in touch with me and let me know how things go," Dr. Hawkins advised.

Suzanne hung up the phone after finishing her conversation with Dr. Hawkins. The appointment with Dr. Mendenhall was now in place, so she felt it was important to follow her instructions to the letter.

She found a lighter buried amongst the clutter of the catch-all drawer in the kitchen and proceeded through the house leaving the glimmer of burning candles in her wake. That part was easy. Candles were always plentiful in their home because both she and Kent loved the air of romance and tranquility the candles provided. Suzanne made her way to the master suite and touched a flame to the last candle that remained unlit on her nightstand and then straightened up to look critically at the image in the mirror over her dresser. She was dressed in black from head to toe. "This will never do," she scolded herself.

Suzanne began by pulling the oversized black T-shirt, which she had "borrowed" from her husband, up over her head and letting it fall in a crumpled heap at her feet. Her faded black jeans joined the pile, along with black knee socks. She stood there for a moment looking at her lacy black bra and matching black satin panties.

"Well, nobody could ever accuse me of not being color co-ordinated," she said, "I wonder if I have to go as far as wearing ugly white underwear. Surely Dr. Mendenhall didn't mean I had to go that far!"

Suzanne turned her attention toward Jake, who was looking up with questioning eyes from under the fluff of his curly, black locks. "You're black and you are a good dog. Aren't you Jake?" Suzanne continued, "It just proves that all things black are not bad."

Poor Jake was looking more confused by the minute. Suzanne reached down to give him a pat on the head and then turned and began rummaging through her dresser drawers in an attempt to find something to wear. It wasn't going to be easy. She rarely bought anything for herself and when she did it was usually something in her favorite color, which just happened to be black. There was an occasional blue or a splash of red, and since Kent came into her life, she had added one or two items of his favorite color, green, but white was not to be found. The reason was simple: she felt white made her look like a much taller, slightly thinner version of the Pillsbury doughboy. White just was not flattering on her large frame. Suzanne finally decided on blue jeans and a blue and green cotton top. She had heard somewhere that green and blue were healing colors, so she felt like she had made a great compromise. No more black, except for her panties. That would be her little secret.

"I know."

Suzanne stopped with a smile. "Of course, you know! I wasn't trying to hide anything from you, but somehow I didn't think it mattered to you. Good grief! I thought you had more important things to worry about than the color of my underwear," Suzanne retorted.

"Or, whether you wear any at all!" The words came to Suzanne like a great, warm, wonderful smile.

Knowing that this impromptu conversation was about to end, Suzanne questioned softly, "Have I told you lately that I love you?"

"Have you remembered lately how much I love you?"

Feeling filled to overflowing with that love, a tear trickled down Suzanne's cheek. "Thank you," she whispered.

Something within the depths of her soul was telling her that she was going to need to remember the love of God more than ever in the weeks to come. It was a feeling that would not be ignored. Although, it would not be until after her visit with Dr. Mendenhall that she would completely understand.

CHAPTER TEN

Suzanne was on her way back. Somewhere, something had gone terribly wrong. In a state of desperation, she was crying out. "God help me! Where are you? Where have you gone?" Tears were streaming down her face, and her hands were gripping the steering wheel as if her life depended on it. "I don't understand! What happened? God? God!" Suzanne screamed anxiously.

"Okay. Calm down!" she told herself as she took a deep breath and began to try to make sense of all that had happened. "You're just letting yourself get worked up over nothing." Suzanne continued to reason aloud, "You know God is here! You know God is right here!"

Suzanne's voice was shaky and the tears were still flowing unheeded, but she began to sing anyway. "Nearer my God...to thee." Her voice cracked and she sobbed loudly, but she didn't stop. "Nearer to thee..." At times like this, even though she was sure she sounded pitiful; singing always seemed to soothe her. If she had been at home, she would have been sitting at her keyboard playing along. She had no real musical talent, but she embraced it anyway, finding comfort and healing within its melodious presence.

Her voice drifted off as she became aware of the other voices in her head. "We're still here! Suzanne, you cannot do what you did today. We know you don't understand now, but maybe one day you will remember! We are not demons or lost souls. We are you!"

"I can't handle this right now! Don't you understand what you are doing to me?" Suzanne snapped.

Her mind began recalling the events of the day. It had begun so well with a clear, beautiful morning, perfect weather for the long drive she had ahead of her. She had left early enough to allow time for the frequent stops she knew she would have to make in order to walk around in an attempt to relieve the stabbing pain in her knees and back that always accompanied her on any road trip. She had planned well and arrived at Dr. Mendenhall's office a half-hour before her appointment time.

She had been so sure that the answer to all her problems would be found within the walls of that elegant office. She had looked around, taking it all in. Dark mahogany tables only served to enhance the tasteful, navy blue, wing-back chairs and settee all upholstered in rich leather. The light gray carpeting stretched throughout the room dipping occasionally beneath a plush oriental rug. Overall, the atmosphere was polished and professional with just a hint of warmth.

Dr. Mendenhall had entered the waiting room as if on cue, right at the appointed time. She had beckoned Suzanne to join her in her office, which was tucked away neatly at the end of a winding hallway. Suzanne lagged behind, each step a painful reminder of the two-hour drive she had just made. Dr. Mendenhall paused in the doorway and turned to watch her approach, waiting patiently as Suzanne finally hobbled past her into the sanctum the office. "I was concerned about you making this trip," Dr. Mendenhall said softly, "I can see that it has taken a toll on you."

"Trust me, if you can help me, all the pain and inconvenience won't matter at all!" Suzanne replied.

"I hope, then, that you won't be disappointed. We have a lot to accomplish in a short amount of time, so it's important that we get started. Find somewhere to sit where you will be comfortable, and then we will begin."

Suzanne scanned the room. It all looked comfortable. Large, cushioned, teal leather chairs and a sofa formed a conversation grouping around an elegant wrought-iron and glass coffee table. Throughout the room, candles flickered and highlighted an array of angel figurines. Scattered among the floral arrangements and photographs that graced the different tables throughout the room, Suzanne could also see a variety of colored crystals, and the walls were adorned with lovely angelic paintings. There was a softness about the entire room that immediately made Suzanne feel at ease. In fact, she was also somewhat amused by the mixture of knick knacks. It was hard to determine whether Dr. Mendenhall was into Christianity or some New Age philosophy.

The pillowed cushions seemed to embrace Suzanne as she sank into the chair nearest to a large picture framed window. The vertical blinds were open just enough to allow her to catch a glimpse of the outside world, but, for that moment, she had given her full attention to the doctor as she began to speak.

"I don't know what your plans are after we are through here, but there is a holistic nurse here in town that may be able to give you some relief from the pain you are experiencing. I have used her myself on several occasions and she has been able to work wonders for me. It's just a suggestion. If you would like, I could contact her and see if she can work you in today." Dr. Mendenhall's tone was gentle and concerned.

"I have never been to anyone like that. My parents are into homeopathic medicine, but that is about the extent of my ventures outside conventional medicine. However, the fact that I am here should tell you that I try not to limit the possibilities. Yes, if you think she could make my trip home a little more bearable, I would like to see her before I leave if you could arrange that," Suzanne replied.

Dr. Mendenhall graciously obliged. Suzanne studied the doctor as she picked up the small phone sitting within reach and began making arrangements. She was thin, almost too thin, and her crisp, white linen suit was tailored to perfection. In contrast, the deep, rich, tones of her hair softened her face and, although her eyes were extremely intense, there was a genuine sincerity in their depths.

"Well, that is taken care of." Dr. Mendenhall smiled at Suzanne. "I will give you directions before you leave so you will be able to find her. Now, we need to move on. Unfortunately, even though Dr. Hawkins and I have discussed your case, I still have a lot of questions I need to ask you. I realize that you have probably answered these same questions several times before, but I assure you they are necessary if I am going to get an accurate perspective on your situation."

The questions continued into the next hour. Suzanne patiently answered each one knowing that within each of her answers the doctor was looking for "the solution" to her problems. All she could do was tell it like it was and hope Dr. Mendenhall could somehow find the key to unlock the madness and set her free. The questions had finally come to a halt and Dr. Mendenhall began to explain that if Suzanne would agree she would put her into a light hypnotic state during which she would ask just a few more questions. Suzanne gave her consent and the doctor began.

"Close your eyes and imagine yourself being surrounded by a white light, a heavenly light. Let the light engulf you. It is a light of protection. Let the light filter through you and fill you. Starting at the top of your head let it flow through you and push the darkness away. Now I am going to begin counting from ten down to one. I want you to completely relax. With each number, release any tension or resistance you may be feeling." Dr. Mendenhall continued to speak softly, pausing briefly between each number. "Ten. You are protected. Nine. You are completely relaxed. Eight. . ."

Suzanne was vaguely aware of Dr. Mendenhall requesting that

she lift a finger to indicate the answer "yes" and another finger to indicate the answer "no." The next moment of lucid recollection had been the beginning of her downward spiral.

Suzanne woke up sobbing uncontrollably. What had happened? Why did she feel like she had lost her best friend? What was wrong?

At this point Dr. Mendenhall was standing behind her and she could hear her softly praying. "Let the light of God surround you. Let His power protect you. Let the presence of God watch over you."

Suzanne's sobs quieted and she could feel a sense of peace, but the emptiness was still there. "What happened?" she questioned as the doctor finished and took her seat adjacent to Suzanne.

"I am sure this could seem just a little bit overwhelming, but it's important that you try to express to me how you are feeling in this moment." Dr. Mendenhall eluded Suzanne's question.

"I don't know. I feel very exhausted, like a wrung out dishrag… and…and…" Suzanne began crying like a wounded child and found herself unable to go on.

Dr. Mendenhall waited quietly as she handed a box of tissues to Suzanne. "It's important that you try to continue."

Suzanne sniffed as she wiped the tears away and then she just blurted it out. "I feel like I have lost a part of me or my best friend! I feel empty and very scared."

"Suzanne, given all that you have been through, this is understandable. I have a copy of a prayer that I would like you to carry with you and repeat at least once a day." Dr. Mendenhall handed a photocopy of the prayer in question toward Suzanne and then continued, "When someone gets used to something over a period of time, it makes sense that when that thing is no longer there, it may be replaced with a feeling of loss, but that usually fades with time."

Suzanne knew what Dr. Mendenhall was trying to say in her own, delicate way. So it was true. She was or had been possessed, or at the very least had an attached spirit. Yet, now that she was face to face with this new reality, something about the diagnosis seemed wrong--very, very wrong! She turned her attention back to Dr. Mendenhall, who had continued to speak.

"Does the name Michael mean anything to you?"

Suzanne paused for a moment and quickly searching for anyone in her past by the name of Michael. "No, there was really only one Michael who had any significance in my life. It was one of those relationships that you thank God never went any further than it did. We were going to get married. What a disaster that would have been! I had been so impressed with the loving relationship Michael seemed to have with his parents that I desperately wanted to know what it was like to be part of a family like that. I imagine, for Michael, it was just a silly case of teenage infatuation. The bottom line is, fortunately, our relationship ended, and to the best of my knowledge, he is happily married to someone else. I haven't thought of him in more than a decade, so it seems really odd that you would bring him up now."

"No, I am pretty sure that your Michael is not the Michael I met today. This Michael was a very small and timid child. He seemed very sad and reluctant to leave. I'm sure that everything is okay now. I only asked because I believe that Michael had been with you for a very long time and I thought you might have been aware of him. You seemed very upset when it came time for him to go into the light. I realize that this whole process may be a little disconcerting for you, but you need to trust me when I say that everything is going to be all right. Dr. Hawkins and I are both here for you every step of the way."

"Thanks, there is definitely comfort in knowing that," Suzanne said quietly.

Dr. Mendenhall smiled warmly and began writing down directions on a piece of notepaper. "The nurse you'll be seeing is Martha McQuinn. She is expecting you in about a half an hour. Don't worry; you'll have plenty of time to get there. Do you think you will be able to understand these directions?" Dr. Mendenhall questioned as she handed the slip of paper to Suzanne.

After looking at the directions briefly, Suzanne confirmed that they were clear enough; she should have no problem finding Nurse McQuinn.

The session with Dr. Mendenhall ended with some last minute instructions from the doctor. "It is important that you surround yourself with light and use the prayer of protection on a daily basis."

Suzanne wound her way through the heavy traffic. Her mind focused on finding her way in a city that was completely unfamiliar to her. However, except for the one time she had to double back because she had missed her exit, Suzanne was able to arrive without incident.

Nurse McQuinn's office was located in an old, rundown section of town. The office itself was in an archaic home that had been renovated to accommodate several small businesses.

Suzanne followed the wrap-around porch toward the back of the house and read the plaques on the doors that announced the name of the business behind it. She was looking for suite 21. As she approached the next door, there was a simple country heart hanging just below the number 21 that said, "Welcome".

Well, here goes nothing, Suzanne thought to herself as she cautiously opened the door. The funny thing about the house/office combination was that she was never sure whether she should knock before entering. However, the friendly smile that greeted her on the other side of the door quickly erased her doubts.

"Suzanne? I've been expecting you!" Martha's brilliant blue eyes were as bright as her smile.

"I really appreciate the way that you worked me into your schedule on such a short notice," Suzanne replied.

"It was really no problem at all. I had planned on taking the afternoon off to get caught up on some paperwork." Martha motioned toward a small desk that was somewhat cluttered with folders and papers. "It's a necessary part of my business but not a part I really enjoy. When Dr. Mendenhall called, I was delighted to have an excuse to break away for an hour or so. You are certainly welcome!"

The room was tiny with a screen divider separating it. One half was dedicated to the small roll-top desk and a couple of wooden chairs. On the other side, Suzanne could see a massage table and, along the wall on each side of a window, two book shelves that were filled with an array of colored bottles and jars, all holding what appeared to be different aromatic oils and herbal remedies. A trail of smoke wafted up from an incense burner and its fragrance pleasantly filled the small room. Orchestra music played softly in the background and the roughly woven rag rugs strewn across the hardwood floor lent the finishing touches to the cozy room.

Suzanne sat on the edge of a somewhat uncomfortable straight back wooden chair. "You may need an extra sheet of paper!" she teased as Martha posed her pen ready to begin writing Suzanne's medical history. "Okay, here goes. I have chondromalacia in both of my knees. In English that means my kneecaps are not centered the way they are supposed to be, so they have run off track my entire life, leading to the complete deterioration of both of my knees. I also suffer from arthritis and fibromyalgia. I have carpal tunnel in both wrists as well as problems with the nerves in my elbows and neck. I also suffer frequently with tension and migraine headaches. Other than that, and the fact that some would tell you I am completely nuts, I am in perfect health." Suzanne ended with an ironic grin.

"Okay, I think I've got all of that." Martha looked up from the form in front of her and proceeded to explain in detail what Suzanne could expect. "If you'll come through here," Martha continued as she led the way to the massage table, "remove your shoes and lie down on your back, we can begin. Just try to relax and make yourself as comfortable as possible."

Suzanne spent the next hour in a state of peaceful rest. She was barely aware of Martha as she moved quietly around the table. A calming nature symphony filled the room accompanied by different aromas that soothed and calmed Suzanne.

Occasionally, Suzanne would peek out from underneath her eyelids to observe Martha moving her hands, in a graceful pattern, just inches above her body. *Very strange!* Suzanne thought to herself. But for the moment, strange or not, it was working.

"We're through now, but you can continue to lie there as long as you like." Suzanne was brought out of the light state of slumber by the gentle voice of Nurse McQuinn.

"Thank you. Wow, that was really relaxing!" Suzanne replied as she sat up and slipped into her clogs. "It would be nice to lay here for another hour or so, but I need to start home. What time is it anyway?"

"It's three thirty."

"Wow, where has the time gone!" Suzanne gasped.

"I had to spend a little more time than usual," Martha smiled.

"I don't understand? Was something wrong?" Suzanne queried.

"Not wrong, necessarily, just a little strange." Martha's voice trailed off as if she was reluctant to continue, but the anxious look on Suzanne's face must have indicated that there was no way she was going to be allowed to stop midstream. "Because you are not familiar with the terminology of my profession, I guess the easiest way to describe it is to say that there was no energy flow. All of the centers were closed. You should feel much better now."

"I see," Suzanne said calmly, "Well, it's a good thing I came then. Thank you." Her smile was sweet and her exit graceful.

Outside Martha's office, Suzanne hurried to her car and tried to ignore the panic that seemed to be stirring like a whirlpool within her. However, the fact that she noticed it at all seemed to strengthen it. The feeling of overwhelming loss was still there, and

Nurse McQuinn's words, "Strange . . . Closed . . . Everything was closed," seemed to undo any peace she may have experienced moments earlier. She was feeling like she had lost a part of her soul and, worse, her connection to God. Something was wrong!

"What went wrong?" Suzanne screamed. "What happened? God? God! Where are you?"

There was no reply, only an eerie silence. Many miles away and over an hour later, she still found no answer to her desperate pleas.

"God?" Suzanne's screams had quieted to a whispered prayer. "Be with me now in this hour of darkness. Hear my cry, dear God! Help me to understand. Please, dear God, I need you now in this hour of despair. God, please! This is not the time for games! I need to know you are here with me! I need to feel your love! I need to hear your voice! Speak to me, dear God, I pray!"

Suzanne continued to pray for the remainder of her journey home. Had she stopped for just a moment to listen, she may have heard God speaking quietly to her heart, but in her fear she had forgotten that one cannot hear unless they listen.

It took every ounce of courage Suzanne had within her to make it through that evening. Thankfully, her thoughtful husband had ordered pizza for supper, so all she really had to do was make small talk until bedtime.

Suzanne had become very adept at masking her inner turmoil over the years, and this was one of those times when she thanked God she was able to do so. If Kent and her children could see past her smile and into the depths of her soul, they would have recoiled in horror. Darkness, despair, fear, and emptiness for which there are no words, regardless of how they are portrayed, do not create a picture of beauty.

Suzanne tried to savor the warmth of the moment as she tucked Tyler and Nicole in for the night. There was nothing quite like feeling their arms wrapped tightly around her neck and their soft, slobbery kisses. The "I love you, Mom!" that always followed was like a huge cherry on top of the most delectable hot fudge sundae. How could she possibly ever ask for anything more? This was bliss, pure, unadulterated joy! To love and be loved without condition, nothing else quite compared.

A gentle smile still touched her lips as she returned to the living room to find Kent completely engrossed in a baseball game that had carried over into extra innings. "So, are the Braves going to win this one?" Suzanne questioned as she bent down to steal a kiss.

"Of course, I've got on my lucky Brave shorts. You know they can't lose when I'm wearing my lucky shorts!" Kent laughed.

"How could I ever doubt the shorts?" Suzanne retorted. "I guess I'm going to go lie down and catch up on some reading. Do you need anything before I settled in?"

"No, I'm fine for now. I'll be there in just a few minutes. This game can't go on too much longer."

Suzanne retreated to her bedroom and began preparing to retire for the evening. She stopped briefly to light the candles on her bedside table and then continued to disrobe. She was still trying to make sense of her day and overcome the emptiness that seemed to penetrate the very core of her being. She absentmindedly slipped a long silk gown over her head and turned toward the mirror to run a brush through the tangles in her hair. "Aw, crap, I put on a black gown again!" Just as she started to reach for another nightgown that would fill the doctor's prescription for her to wear light colors Suzanne suddenly stopped herself. "That's it! I have had it! I am through!" Suzanne screamed silently. "All right, God, it's just you and me, and I've got something to say and you better be listening. I have spent years of my life living with this inner turmoil and I refuse to let it go on any longer! Everything I have done in attempt to rid myself of this darkness has only created more fear and more frustration. Good grief, to be afraid of a stupid color... that is just going way too far! Do you remember that mouse? That stupid little mouse! There I was lying in bed in that old rundown cottage that had no cupboards listening to that mouse rummaging around in my cookies. The longer I lay there and listened to it, the bigger I imagined it was. When I finally found the courage to get up and set a trap I saw that it had dragged that big Heyday cookie across the counter, and in my mind the mouse grew a few more inches. Instead of one, I set three traps and surrounded that cookie. Remember? The next morning the cookie was gone, the cheese from the traps was gone, and there was no mouse. I tried to catch that silly mouse for over a week, and every morning, when I awoke to find the cheese missing from the traps, the mouse became even larger and smarter in my mind. I was convinced I was sharing my cottage with a humungous rat that had the intelligence of Einstein. I was on the verge of moving out and letting that darn mouse have the cottage, but then I finally outsmarted the little turd with a liberal dose of peanut butter. He looked so innocent lying there in that trap--the teeniest, tiniest, mouse I had ever seen! Talk about making a mountain out of a mole hill!"

"Thank you for remembering."

"You're back!" Suzanne exclaimed.

"I am always here. I never left."

"Well you could have let me know! I needed you! I really needed you! Don't you understand?"

"Yes, I understand. You were afraid that you had lost me. You feared I wasn't there for you. You created a very big rat, my child."

"Are you telling me that my fear blocked my communication with you?"

"Fear as you know it has been known to create many obstacles."

"I remember something Dr. Hawkins told me once. She said that there are really only two emotions, love and fear, and every other emotion is rooted in or a result of love or fear. It is all starting to make sense now. I mean, I look around at the racism and ethnic cleansing and I realize the root of those actions is fear.

Those people are actually afraid of being contaminated by or of losing power to another race. My father is afraid of being wrong, so he refuses to apologize for any of his actions no matter how horrific they are. My mother is afraid she won't be loved so she works herself to death trying to please everyone around her. There are those who fear hunger so they hoard and others who fear discomfort or disease so they distance themselves from those who need their help and love the most. Those afraid of being poor become greedy. We all act and react based on our fears. The man who brutally killed the gay man because he propositioned him was afraid of being loved in the wrong way and he rationalized it by saying the Bible says it's wrong to be gay. However, in his fear, he seemed to forget that that same book also said, 'Thou shall not kill' and 'love your neighbor as you do yourself,' or that 'love covers a multitude of sins.' We all do a lot of stupid things because we are afraid. I guess I just never realized how silly most of my fears were until now. Okay, that's it; I'm going to try not to be afraid anymore. Thank you! I feel like a weight has been lifted. I feel free!"

"You are. Free to be. Free to create. Try to always be love and not to create any more big rats."

"Right. Hey, you caused me to remember that story!" Suzanne said accusingly. "You were talking to me all along."

"Always."

CHAPTER ELEVEN

It occurred to Suzanne sometime later that in all of her many conversations with God, she had never asked for an explanation or the reason for her many mental and physical malfunctions. She had repeatedly asked for help in dealing with them or found herself begging to be fixed on many occasions, but never once did she ask, "Would you mind explaining me to me?"

Why, in fact, was she spending hundreds of dollars on psychotherapy when it could be as simple as going to the source, the Creator of this madness she knew herself to be? Perhaps there was a simple explanation. Could it be that just once God had screwed up, maybe crossed a wire or two when she was created?

"No. Try again." The answer came soft and sweet.

"I am tired of trying to figure this puzzle out. How about just giving it to me straight and putting me out of my misery?" Suzanne retorted.

"It's rather simple actually. I am all that is and therefore you are all that is and the creator of all you know to be."

"So, this flawed me is your, um, my creation?" Suzanne questioned tentatively.

"Yes! Isn't it perfect?"

"Perfect? Perfect! What do you mean, perfect? Look at me! I

am a mess!" The frustration was clear in Suzanne's voice.

"There are many things you wanted to know that could not be experienced in what your society deems to be a 'flawless body' or a 'sane mind,' and so I/you/we created Suzanne. When what you know yourself to be no longer serves you, then you will create a different version of you."

"A new, improved, more perfect, version?" Suzanne queried.

"No, just different. You are already perfect."

"Of course, you are, therefore I am, blah, blah, blah. I get that, but I still don't get me!"

"That is because you see yourself as separate from me. You do not understand the oneness of all that is, but, ironically, you have created a version of yourself that is a flawless picture of me."

"How's that?"

"Well, you call yourself Suzanne and you refer to me as God when, in fact, there are not two of me. Do you remember how the truck driver in Las Vegas called you Lisa when you only knew yourself to be Suzanne?"

"Yes! About that, what was that?" Suzanne's recollection of those lost days made her more determined than ever to get to the bottom of this once and for all.

Suddenly, Suzanne's mind was flooded with memories from her childhood of similar misplaced moments in time. How could she forget seeing those angry scratches across her father's face? However, when she had questioned him, asking how the scratches had gotten there, he had become enraged. "You! I promise you will never do it again!" He shouted with his fist clenched and his nostrils flaring like an enraged bull.

Many times, Suzanne had awoken battered, bruised, curled up in a fetal position, and hidden behind a wall of hay bales in the barn or under her bed, but she could never remember how she, with her many wounds, had gotten there. Afterwards, it was as if a stronger version of herself had taken over and efficiently went about doing whatever was necessary to cover up and disguise any signs that something horrific must have occurred.

Since Suzanne's eighteenth birthday, when her Dad's gift to her was a boot to the curb, the incidences of those lost moments had become rare. Looking back through the years, she could only recall two times, or possibly two-and-a-half if she wanted to count that one time she had tried to write a check at the local store. It was almost as if she had been stranger observing herself become a child who had absolutely no idea what a check was, let alone how to fill one out and then, suddenly, there was another shift. She had seen a tall, very intelligent looking gentleman in a black tailored suit step in and fill the check out. As Suzanne observed, her only thought was, "there is no way that check will ever make it through the bank because that is definitely not my handwriting."

Other than that, there were only two other times. One was when Suzanne was living in Florida and the abuse from her first husband, Wade, had pushed her to the point of suicide and somehow, without any recollection of how it occurred, she had managed to end up in Las Vegas. The other happened that painful night when Suzanne had volleyed in and out of oblivion as she tried to get home from her doctor's visit. It seemed clear that in both of those incidences she had been pushed to a breaking point on both a mental and physical level.

So, what answers were meant to fill all those missing blanks? Could they be so dreadful Suzanne had blocked them out completely? That seemed plausible, but then there was "Lisa" in Las Vegas and Dr. Mendenhall had mentioned a "Michael" that day in New Orleans when she felt like she had lost a part of herself. Is that what God meant? Were Lisa and Michael a part of her, Suzanne, that did not see themselves as connected but as separate entities entirely?

Almost immediately, the voices began in unison. "You are remembering us Suzanne!"

"Remembering who? Who are you?" Suzanne demanded.

Suzanne felt a change come over her and, almost immediately, it was as if she was outside her body once again observing. A young man in his twenties stepped forward. "It's me, John," he said in a quiet voice, "I am the one who is constantly seeking for truth when it comes to God and religion. Remember, you wanted to know how a bad daddy could be loved by God. You said that if I could figure out how it was possible for God to love daddy, then maybe you could love him too. I help you love and forgive those who have harmed you."

Ah, so you're the reason why I seem to go from raving heathen to saint almost instantaneously, Suzanne thought to herself.

"Heathen? That would be me, Candy." Suzanne watched her body take on a sultry pose. "I am your wild child, honey, your rebel, the one who refuses to be fenced in by anything or anyone. You love me and you know it."

There was a pause and then a very insolent girl in her teens stepped forward. "Candy you are so dumb! I am the one Suzanne loves the most. I am her best friend. I know everything about her. You remember me, right Suzanne? It's Angelica, your BFF, and it's a good thing too because you have really done some stupid things. If it wasn't for me, you would be dead! Remember when you tried not to cry when Daddy beat you? You wanted him to realize how strong you were, so you let Michael help you. Well, I made Michael cry because if he didn't cry you would be dead! Do you understand? Dead, dead, dead! Good thing I am the brains of this operation 'cause you can really be dumb! Well, maybe not so much lately, but you are lazy as hell. I don't care if you are hurting; you need to do more and you need to be tough, like me." Angelica finally stopped raving long enough to catch her breath. "Oh look, Michael, stupid Michael is here!"

Suzanne watched herself go into the fetal position and the small, frail, and very timid boy slowly began to speak. "Hi. . . I think you are very smart Suzanne. I don't like Angelica. You and I promised we wouldn't cry and then Angelica said I have to. She's a big meanie! I love you, Suzanne, but I really, really hate Daddy!

It's okay. You don't have to hate him too. I can hate him enough for both of us. That way you don't have to go to hell for hating him. You are a good girl, Suzanne. Daddy is the bad one! I hope he goes to hell and burns up so he can't hurt us anymore! Oh yeah, and don't worry, I am very good at hiding just in case that doctor lady wants to try to get rid of me some more."

Suzanne was torn between trying to take control of this situation or letting what seemed to be occurring run its course. It was as if she had opened a photo album of days gone by and was suddenly forced to relive pieces of her past that had faded completely from mind. While there was a certain amount of excitement at the discovery of this forgotten past, Suzanne was acutely aware that there was a reason it had been buried so carefully. And so it was with complete trepidation that she allowed it all to continue.

One by one, they filed in. The intelligent gentleman who wrote the check that day at the store introduced himself as Charles. He was a bit of a control freak, constantly checking and rechecking, making sure everything was in order at all times, because one small thing out of place could have sent her father into a rage.

Lisa was the dreamer and a very good actress who had been able to manipulate her way out of many adverse situations. Lisa had high hopes for her future and had been the one who made her way to Vegas.

Rose, the gentle healer, came forward next. Her entire presence exuded love and, like a warm blanket, it wrapped around Suzanne, embracing her, comforting her, warming her.

Finally, there was William. He did not come quietly. It was as if a small explosion occurred upon his arrival. He was big and bad and mad as hell! "What? You don't remember me, your garbage dump! All your anger, all your resentment, all your frustration, you gave it all to me! You want me to grow fricken roses with this shit! Fuck you! I protected you! I fought back for you, and now you want to tuck me away in some small corner as if I don't exist anymore! Damn you!"

Suzanne's fist slamming through the glass top coffee table jolted her back. As she ran for the bathroom cupping one hand under the other to catch the blood dripping from it in a steady stream, her mind went into overdrive. She could easily explain away the coffee table to Kent. She had just tripped on the rug, or something, and fallen into it. But this? This! What the hell was all of this? John? Candy? Angelica? How many were there? Where did they come from? Where did they go? How in God's name... *God? God!*

"Interesting, hmm?"

"Um, that is not exactly the word I would use to describe it!" Suzanne retorted.

"What word then?"

"Nuts! Total and utter fricken nuts!" She was screaming at the top of her lungs at this point.

"Quite a mixed bag of nuts you created then!"

How could God be laughing at her at a time like this?

How? Suzanne took a deep breath and tried to calm herself, and then suddenly she found herself laughing too. It was a wry chuckle at first, and then, as she began to think about it, the more amused she became. "So, I, we did this to me?" she questioned.

"Very creative and quite an experience, hmm?"

"That's probably an understatement," Suzanne replied with an ironic grin. "Now what? What in the world am I supposed to do now?"

Like a child who had just impulsively knocked over the largest tower of blocks they had ever built because something inside of them knew the next version would be even grander, Suzanne stood there, a silent witness to the crumpled heap of madness.

◢◢◢

If you enjoyed this book, there is a sequel being written entitled, *A New Creation.*

www.ingramcontent.com/pod-product-compliance
Lightning Source LLC
Chambersburg PA
CBHW020243290526
45784CB00003B/1086